PROFESSIONAL CHOICES: VALUES AT WORK

ANN A. ABBOTT

PROFESSIONAL CHOICES:

VALUES AT WORK

National Association of Social Workers, Inc.
Silver Spring, MD 20910

Copyright © 1988 by the National Association of Social Workers, Inc.

All rights reserved. No part of this book may be reproduced or transmitted in any form or by any means, electronic or mechanical, including photocopying, recording, or by any information storage and retrieval system, without permission in writing from the publisher.

Library of Congress Cataloging-in-Publication Data

Abbott, Ann Augustine, 1943–
  Professional choices.

  1. Social work education—United States. 2. Social workers—United States—Attitudes. 3. Professional socialization. I. Title.
HV11.A19 1988   361.3   87-34901
ISBN 0-87101-159-X

Printed in the United States of America

*This book is dedicated to my mother,
Ethel Denys Augustine,
whose values are reflected in her
inner serenity and caring, vivacious smile.*

Contents

Illustrations
ix

Tables
x

Foreword
xiii

Preface
xiv

O·N·E
Socialization: The Road to Professional Identity
1

T·W·O
Professional Opinion Scale: Determining Professional Socialization in Light of Value Orientation
20

T·H·R·E·E
Choice: The Selection of a Profession
31

F·O·U·R
Education: Its Contribution to Professional Socialization
47

F·I·V·E
Time in the Trenches: Orientation of Seasoned Professionals
64

S·I·X
Demographics: Political Philosophy, Geography, Social Class, Religion, Gender, and Age
87

S·E·V·E·N
Marketplace: A Comparison of Administrators and Direct Practitioners
99

E·I·G·H·T
Socialization, Life Experience, and Value Orientation: Their Influence on Social Work Practice
106

A·P·P·E·N·D·I·X A
Professional Opinion Scale: An Instrument for Determining Value Orientation
115

A·P·P·E·N·D·I·X B
Professional Opinion Scale
147

About the Author
163

Illustrations

Figure 1	Value, Attitude, Opinion Hierarchy, and Classification Scheme	4
Figure 2	Hierarchical Relationship between Values, Ethics, and Moral Decision Making	6
Figure 3	Box-Plots for Value Scores of Beginning Undergraduate Students	39
Figure 4	Box-Plots for Value Scores of Beginning Graduate Students	40
Figure 5	Box-Plots for Value Scores of Graduates of Undergraduate Professional Programs	53
Figure 6	Box-Plots for Value Scores of Graduates of Graduate Professional Programs	54
Figure 7	Box-Plots for Value Scores of Seasoned Professionals	77

Appendix A

Figure A-1	Box-Plots for Value Scores by Respondent Type	122

Tables

Table 1	Public Policy Statements of NASW: Topic and Date	24
Table 2	Mean POS Value Scores of Beginning Undergraduate and Graduate Students	37
Table 3	Significant Differences between Means of Beginning Social Work and Other Professional Students Based on Tukey's Honestly Significant Difference	38
Table 4	POS Value Score Means for 1986 Graduates Representing Each Professional Group	55
Table 5	Significant Differences between Means of Social Work and Other Professions (1986 Graduates) Based on Tukey's Honestly Significant Difference	55
Table 6	Comparison of Group Value Means for Beginning Social Work Students, Recent Graduates, Faculty, Field Instructors, and Agency Personnel	58
Table 7	Comparison of Value Scores of Beginning Students and Graduates with Each Other and with Faculty, Field Instructors, and Social Service Agency Personnel	59
Table 8	Mean POS Value Scores of Seasoned Professionals by Professional Type	76
Table 9	Significant Differences between Means of Social Workers and Other Seasoned Professionals Based on Tukey's Honestly Significant Difference	78
Table 10	ANOVAs of Value 1 Scores by Profession and Point in Professional Career	79
Table 11	ANOVAs of Value 2 Scores by Profession and Point in Professional Career	80
Table 12	ANOVAs of Value 3 Scores by Profession and Point in Professional Career	80
Table 13	ANOVAs of Value 4 Scores by Profession and Point in Professional Career	81
Table 14	Specific Sample Characteristics ($n = 1,890$)	90
Table 15	Variables Selected by Stepwise Multiple Regression for Predicting Value Scale Scores	93

Table 16	POS Value Score Means for Direct Practitioners and Social Work Administrators	102
Table 17	Summary of Correlations between Political Philosophy and Professional Type	110

Appendix A

Table A-1	General Characteristics of the Three Pilot Samples	126
Table A-2	Specific Characteristics of the Pilot Samples	126
Table A-3	Items Comprising the Four POS Value Dimensions	128
Table A-4	Comparison of Factor Loadings on Value Dimension Items	130
Table A-5	POS Value Subscale Reliability Coefficients	131
Table A-6	Comparision of Value Scores for Various Respondent Types	131
Table A-7	Summary of ANOVAs on Value Scores by All Respondent Types	132
Table A-8	Significant Differences between Respondent Types Based on Tukey's Honestly Significant Difference	132
Table A-9	Results of Analysis of Covariance of Respondent Type on Value Scores, Controlling for the Influence of Various Demographic Variables	133
Table A-10	Factor Loadings on Value Scale Items for Various Respondent Types	134
Table A-11	POS Subscale Reliability Coefficients for Various Respondent Types	135
Table A-12	Comparison of Value Means Based on Sample Factor Loadings for the Three Pilot Samples	136
Table A-13	Summary of ANOVAs in Value Scores of Beginning Students by Profession and Educational Level	136
Table A-14	Summary of Chi-Square Values for Demographic Variables and Professional Type at the Beginning Student Level	136
Table A-15	Results of Analyses of Covariance of Beginning Student Respondent Type on Value Scores, Controlling for the Influence of Various Demographic Variables	137
Table A-16	Summary of ANOVAs in POS Value Score Means by Profession and Educational Level for 1986 Graduates	138

Table A-17	Summary of Chi-Square Values for Demographic Variables and Profession for Recent Graduates	139
Table A-18	Summary of Analyses of Covariance of Graduate Professional Type on Value Scores, Controlling for the Influence of Various Demographic Variables	139
Table A-19	Summary of Chi-Square Values Examining Demographic Variables by Professional Type	141
Table A-20	Summary of ANOVAs in Value Scores of Seasoned Professionals	141
Table A-21	Results of Analyses of Covariance of Seasoned Professionals on Value Scores, Controlling for the Influence of Various Demographic Variables	141
Table A-22	Results of Two-Way ANOVAs by Profession and Point in Professional Career (Time)	142
Table A-23	Correlation Coefficients between Key Demographic Variables	143
Table A-24	Summary of ANOVAs of Value Scores for Social Work Administrators and Direct Practitioners	144
Table A-25	Results of Analyses of Covariance of Social Work Administrators and Direct Practitioners on Value Scores, Controlling for the Influence of Various Demographic Variables	144

Foreword

It is most appropriate that the National Association of Social Workers (NASW) bring *Professional Choices: Values at Work* to the profession and to the community at large. First, the Professional Opinion Scale used by Ann Abbott in her research is based on public policy statements that have been approved by the NASW Delegate Assembly over the years. Policy statements, which may be submitted by any NASW member or group of NASW members, are circulated widely for comments and revisions before they are considered by the assembly. The final published statements demonstrate the depth of concern social workers have for the general welfare of society.

Second, NASW is a product of the profession's commitment to service. NASW was established to further the effectiveness of social work practice and to improve conditions of life for all members of a democratic society. The development of social work practice to meet human needs and the promotion of social action on behalf of human beings have been incorporated into the NASW bylaws. Members subscribe to a code of ethics that mandates adherence to the values and principles of the profession.

Further, NASW is committed to advancing the knowledge base of the profession by publishing sound works drawn from social work research and practice. *Professional Choices: Values at Work* demonstrates clearly and scientifically that social workers as a group are different from other professionals. Social workers place great importance on individual freedom, self-determination, and cultural diversity. They work actively to promote the well-being of others, and they are deeply aware of the need to protect the rights of others.

We hope that individual social workers will find an affirmation of their beliefs in this study. In addition, we highly recommend this book for curriculum planning, accreditation reviews, and coursework.

SUZANNE DWORAK-PECK, ACSW
President

MARK G. BATTLE, ACSW
Executive Director

May 1988

Preface

To neglect the importance of values in determining behavior would be akin to denying the importance of muscular structure in relation to physical ability or diet in relation to physical health. What one believes in or values ultimately influences how one acts, just as one's physical strength determines one's physical limitations and one's underlying physical features determine the direction of one's life. For example, a 6-foot, 8-inch person does not choose or qualify to become a jockey, nor does a 4-foot, 10-inch, 110-pound male become an international basketball star. In a similar vein, underlying predispositions and values frequently determine the quality and direction of human interaction.

The question examined here focuses on the extent to which values determine choice of profession, and the extent to which those values can be refined or influenced by that professional choice. This is especially critical in a time marked by increased conservatism and a heightened emphasis on individuals. My basic concern, as a social work practitioner, educator, curriculum development specialist, and active member of the two major professional associations for social workers—the National Association of Social Workers and the Council on Social Work Education—is uncovering the extent to which social workers are different from members of other professions. Have we as a profession been able to maintain our position as social reformers, as conscience setters, as conveyors of social responsibility, and as protectors of clients' rights, especially during a time when being socially responsible does not appear to connote the same prestige and valor it did 15 to 20 years ago? Are social workers different from the general pool of professionals? If so, in what ways are social workers different?

These questions are raised consistently by social work students, prospective students, colleagues, antagonists, politicians, and friends—to name but a few. Just how does a social worker differ from a lawyer? Are social workers really psychologists? Why doesn't a nurse do the job of a social worker? As a professional, I always have resorted to "textbook" answers that accentuate the importance of skills, values, and knowledge; however, I have never been able to substantiate the differences and similarities I pour forth, especially in the area of values. It was my goal when embarking on this book to provide a stronger base for verifying value differences among the professions at various points of career development.

Because of the help of many fellow professionals, friends, and other interested and supportive people, I was able to undertake and complete this project. Members of all the professions examined participated—doctors, lawyers, businesspeople, nurses, educators, psychologists, and, of course, social workers. I personally wish to thank everyone—all 2,328 of you—who completed the Professional Opinion Scale (POS). In addition, I am extremely grateful to everyone who helped with the development of the scale, assisted with its distribution, and reviewed earlier drafts of the manuscript. My special thanks go to the following friends and colleagues who were extremely helpful in significant ways: Dolores Broberg, Merle Broberg, Nancy Buck, Rose Anne Carter, and Andrew Fussner for their help in the refinement of POS; Helen Rosen and Deborah Shapiro for their help with scale refinement, as well as for reading earlier drafts of the manuscript, a role also undertaken by Ludwig Geismar, Lilliam Kingsbury, and Bill Whitlow; Betty Lee Davis for her role in the refinement of POS and her involvement in its distribution; Ronald Mark, J. Gregg Miller, Mary Falck-Miller, Allen Orr, Dale E. Waldkirch, and Myles Wilson for their strong support and help in distribution of the scale; and Paree Stolis and Elizabeth Plofker for their assistance in determining that POS items adequately reflect the content of their source, the NASW Public Social Policy Statements. Without their help, and the help of the many instructors and university officials who facilitated data collection, this project would not have been possible.

I also am extremely grateful to Rutgers–The State University of New Jersey, and all the individuals from that institution who were instrumental in my obtaining faculty leave time for development of POS and initial collection of data. I am especially thankful to the computer center staff on the Camden campus for their assistance and unending good will. Above all, I owe thanks to my intellectual partner, friend, and husband, Arthur C. Huntley, who provided encouragement, insight, and support, and who never for a moment doubted that this book would come to completion and meaningful fruition.

O · N · E

Socialization:
The Road to Professional Identity

◆

Although social work researchers have attempted to examine the value base of the social work profession during the past 25 years, little attention has been directed toward professional values of the eighties, a time marked by a resurgence of national conservatism and a rise in individualism. As best-selling author John Naisbitt so aptly noted in *Megatrends,* "During the 1970s, Americans began to disengage from the institutions that had disillusioned them and to relearn the ability to take action on their own . . . reclaiming America's traditional sense of self-reliance after four decades of trusting in institutional help."[1] This resurgence of a focus on self-help or privatization of help appears to represent a major reversal in philosophy—from one based on social responsibility and the Judeo-Christian ethic to that of earlier times founded on social Darwinism and the Protestant ethic.[2]

Another popular writer, George Gilder, reinforces this philosophical shift in *Wealth and Poverty* by advocating the extension to the poor of the freedoms and opportunities necessary to achieve wealth.[3] This is in lieu of giving direct financial help to counter poverty; his contention is that such financial help negates the incentive to change. Many people recognize that his theory is akin to dangling a carrot in front of a paraplegic who is located without means of transportation at the far end of a football field. That efforts such as Proposition 13 have received such strong support, however, clearly indicates that a significant number of voters condone the reduction of institutional support for the poor.[4] Opponents of Gilder's theory argue that he based his reasoning on spurious or false relationships, not taking intervening variables into account, but the fact remains that the argument is not strong enough to convince the opposition. Although reduction of monetary support is evident throughout the system, an increase in rights and opportunities is not.[5] In fact, evidence to the contrary is paramount, with decreased funding and increased censorship in such areas as abortion and education (for example, Scopes II in Tennessee).

In Scopes II (won October 24, 1986), fundamentalist Christian parents filed a lawsuit against Hawkins County, Tennessee, public schools, stating that the schools "violated 1st Amendment rights of certain pupils to exercise religious freedom by using textbooks which asserted beliefs contrary to the students' religious beliefs." The court found nothing wrong with the books; the judge ruled against forced reading by all students. The series of books published by Holt, Rinehart, and Winston was currently in use in more than 15,000 districts across the country. The parents who filed the lawsuit protested that such books as the *Wizard of Oz* "promoted an anti-Christian, atheistic philosophy of 'secular humanism.' Some of the objectionable themes cited included sun worship, internationalism, and one-world government."[6]

As these general societal changes occur, there is a great need to determine the impact such changes have had on professional ideologies. As recently as 1984, Loewenberg noted that one of the most urgent needs of the profession of social work is the clarification of its underlying ideology.[7] In light of current philosophical trends, it is critical to determine whether the sociopolitical biases or values normally attributed to social work professionals are truly held by them. If they are not, then what is the true value orientation of members of the social work profession? To facilitate successful collaboration, it is important not only to determine the value orientation of social workers but also to determine how that orientation compares with that of members of other professions—specifically, law, medicine, psychology, education, nursing, and business. Educators and professionals assume that the social work educational process and its accompanying socialization have a definite impact on the value assimilation process. To overlook an examination of that impact or the influence of professional experience would be foolhardy, as it would to overlook the role of such significant personal dimensions as gender, race, political party affiliation, political philosophy, religion, family orientation, socioeconomic status (SES), and age.

This work was undertaken with the intent of developing a greater understanding of the current value orientation of the social work profession in relation to that of the larger professional community. Although professional values have been defined as being separate from personal values, the two are intertwined. Although social workers have been identified as espousing a particular stance toward human distress, they are part of the mainstream of society and cannot help but be influenced by the overall philosophical trends prevalent within that society. To what extent they are influenced remains to be determined by this work.

Value, not fact, is the currency of the realm. [One should not] neglect the importance of values for motivating a society.
—R. B. Reich, *Tales of a New America*
(New York: Times Books, 1987), p. xii.

To understand professional behavior, the relationship between values and behaviors must be described, as well as the relationship between values and ethics and the resulting rules designed to govern professional behavior. A description of the development of moral decision making is necessary, together with an understanding of the role professional socialization plays in the development of professional identity. Additional clarification should be gained from a summary of the profession's historical interest in values, along with a summary of the impact professional education has on value assimilation. A description of the general demeanor of contemporary society also should shed some light on current trends in professional values.

Values and Behavior: Their Relationship

Values and behavior are related. Underlying values guide or help to determine behavior. Values governing general behavior are greatly determined by life experiences—familial, cultural, religious, and educational. Professional values, which build upon but go beyond general values, purportedly are influenced by professional education, socialization, and work experience. To a large extent, professional values are delineated by the major organizations representing the profession—in this case, the National Association of Social Workers (NASW) and the Council on Social Work Education (CSWE). Although values are powerful, relatively fixed determinants of behavior, they certainly are not stagnant. Life experiences and the general tenor of society modify basic values, just as educational and professional practice experiences mold one's professional ideology.

Values have been defined by social scientists as "the central organizing principle[s] of any society"[8]; "what is regarded as good and desirable . . . [as] preferred"[9]; "preferred conceptions of people, . . . outcomes for people, . . . instrumentalities for dealing with people"[10]; and "conception[s], explicit or implicit, distinctive of an individual or . . . group, of the desirable which influences the selection from available modes, means, and ends to action."[11] While values, in fact, may be all those things, the only avenue for their measurement is in actual choices or projected choices of behavior.[12]

Meddin developed a classification scheme that clearly delineates the relationship between values and behavior.[13] Values represent the underlying philosophy or the most abstract level of influence. The more specific, measurable aspects of values are attitudes and, much more so, opinions and actions. Thus, Meddin's hierarchical continuum ranges from values to behavior, from the abstract to the specific, or to what is more suitable for measurement (Figure 1). Florence Kluckhohn and Fred Stodbeck have rephrased Meddin's scheme as moving from knowing to feeling to acting—from existential beliefs to sentiments to actions.[14]

According to Meddin, primary values serve as organizing umbrellas for many subordinate attitudes or opinions.[15] Based on this perspective, a series of attitudes represent specific dimensions of general overriding values. The attitudes, at first glance, may seem unrelated; yet an overriding value may

Figure 1.
Value, Attitude, Opinion Hierarchy, and Classification Scheme

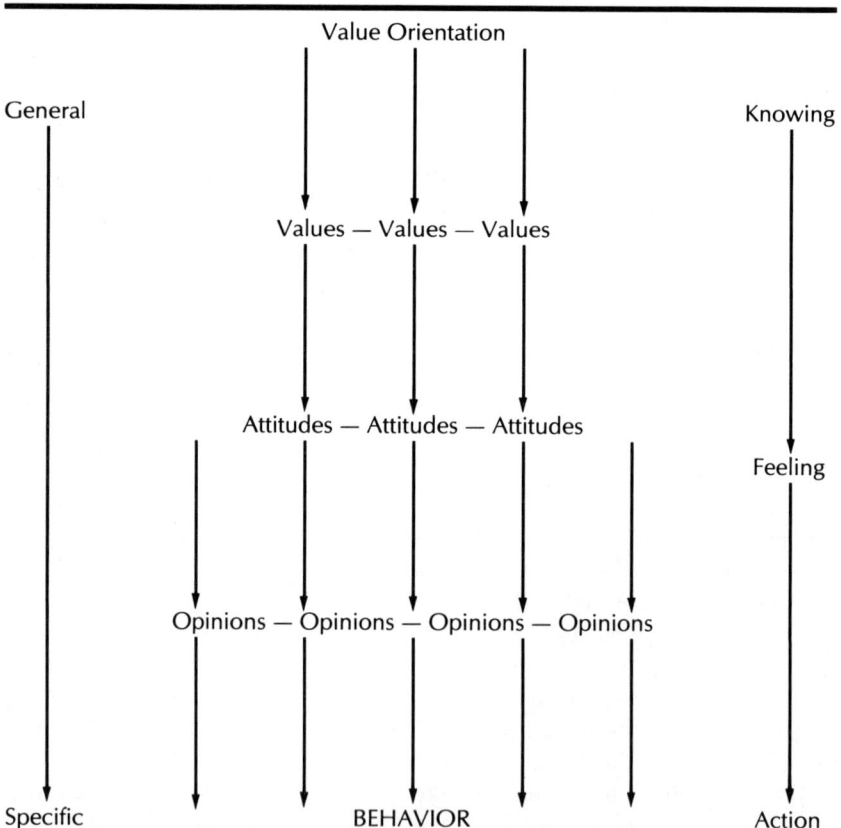

tie the attitudes together. For example, the value of justice or freedom for all may generate an attitude of strong opposition to capital punishment, as well as an attitude against urban families' owning dogs (necessitating a restriction on the animals' free rein to maintain safety). The preceding should hold true for professional values, all of which encompass and nurture a series of subordinate attitudes or opinions. It is at the level of opinions and attitudes within the described scheme that the current study endeavored to identify the current, underlying value umbrellas or primary professional ideology of social work.

Ethics and Values: Their Relationship

In everyday life, personal values and the societal codes governing behavior may be quite divergent; in professional life, professional values and the professional code of ethics are much more congruent and compatible. Societal values influence personal values, and both societal values and personal values influence professional values; thus, none of them is mutually exclusive. Compton and Galaway have noted this relationship: "The social work profession exists within a larger cultural context; it identifies and operationalizes value premises already existing in society and not held exclusively by the profession."[16] Additionally, Compton and Galaway cite Schwartz, who contends that while professional values reflect the norms of the overall society, they also reflect the function of the social service agency and the service contract dimensions necessitated by particular client situations in social service.[17] In other words, professional values reflect both societal *and* professional concerns.

The focus of values is on what is preferable and desirable. Values tend to reflect what *is* in society. Professional values tend to reflect how a profession perceives itself. Ethics, on the other hand, are concerned with what is right and correct.[18] Values do not necessarily guarantee moral behavior or even legally acceptable behavior. Ethics, which grow out of the value base, are designed to delineate the difference between right and wrong. Ethics, like values, do not guarantee moral behavior; however, ethics do set the stage for professional reprimand for immoral or unethical action.

Ethical imperatives flow from that set of basic professional values.[19] The ethical imperatives give way to principles of practice (or guidelines to be applied to practice), which lead to a set of rules or commands (code of ethics) governing professional behavior and ultimately determining professional action (Figure 2). This format parallels the value hierarchy defined by Meddin.[20] Thus, it is through examination of the more measurable—the rules, the opinions, the resulting behavioral choices—that the nature of the underlying value scheme or overall morality of the profession can be determined.

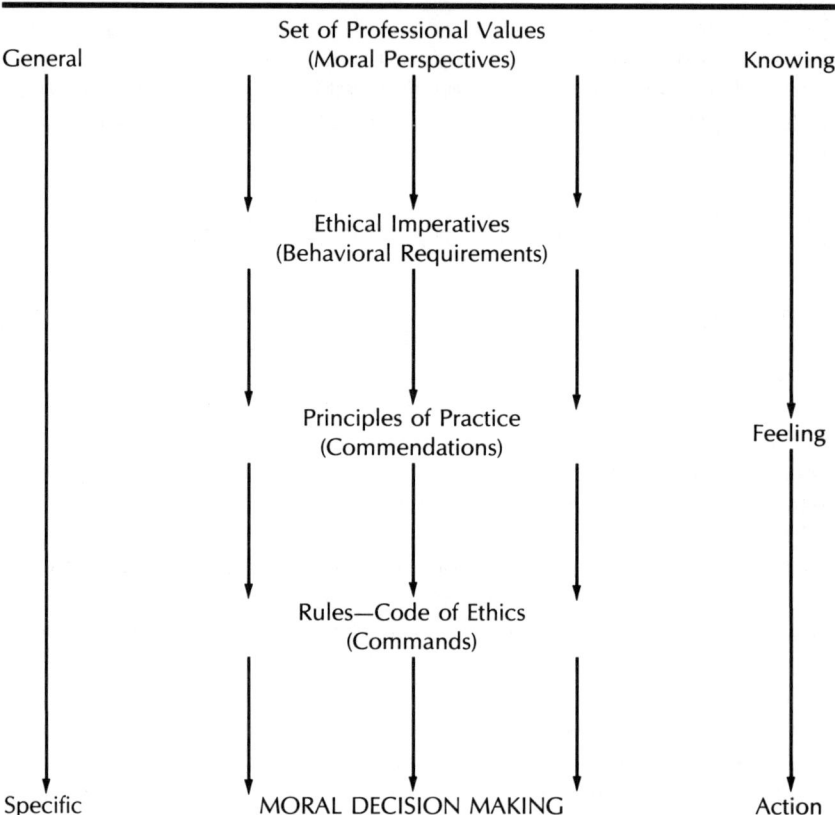

Figure 2.
Hierarchical Relationship between Values, Ethics, and Moral Decision Making

Development of the Moral Frame of Reference

Early educational philosophers, such as Durkheim, have identified the importance of education in the assimilation or development of values and morality.[21] Durkheim implied that the mind is like wax in which the values of the society can be embedded. Through basic education, the student learns the "collective consciousness," or what society expects. Through professional education or socialization, the student learns the morality of his or her chosen profession, or what is expected by that profession. In both, the student supposedly becomes aware of the importance of the underlying value scheme. In general education, that value base reflects the general values of society, which are life, liberty, and the pursuit of happiness. In the profession, the value base reflects values specific to the profession, such as social responsibility, clients' rights, and respect for diversity; the values specific to the profession encompass many of the basic societal values.

How does one learn to incorporate basic values and the accompanying ethical principles into one's thinking? Lawrence Kohlberg, one of the foremost modern authorities on moral education, reaffirmed this process. He contended that education goes beyond the mere learning of rules. In his theory of *cognitive-developmental learning,* a dialectical style of interaction in which ideas and values are modified with each successive experience, he contended that rather than merely accepting the values of parents or teachers, children move beyond them[22] and learn to take others into account. They see that decision making progresses from a morality of constraint (rigid rules) to one of cooperation. Societal (normative) values become superordinate to personal preferences or family values. At this point, students are able "to embrace ideologies, challenge the status quo, envision a better world."[23] In a professional vein, students do not merely comply with the restrictions defined by the code of ethics, but become committed to the underlying value base from which those rules emerge.

This latter level of functioning usually occurs in adolescence; however, Kohlberg cautioned that few actually reach this level of sophistication, or what social workers might refer to as "altruism."[24] Gilligan has strongly criticized Kohlberg's theoretical framework inasmuch as he based his theory on results from 84 males whose development he followed over a 20-year period. Gilligan has noted evidence that women tend to operate at what Kohlberg referred to as lower stages of development. Women, for example, tend to function at stage 3. Gilligan writes, "At this stage morality is conceived in interpersonal terms and goodness is equated with helping and pleasing others."[25] The highest stages (5 and 6) focus on rules to universal principles of justice. The preceding, coupled with their frequently concomitant responsibility for their own children, as well as (until relatively recently) much poorer opportunities for promotion and education, may explain why most female social workers are involved in direct practice (helping others) rather than research and administration, which go beyond policy tasks that involve a greater emphasis on universal principles of justice. As reported by Gilligan, Kohlberg and Kramer contended that once women enter traditionally male areas of work, they recognize the inadequacy of stage 3 and move to higher levels of functioning (stages 5 and 6).[26]

Professional social work behavior requires a broad social and altruistic scope. It thus becomes necessary for social work educators, including field instructors, not only to impart basic rules of the profession, but also, and more important, to foster development and appreciation of this larger perspective, a prerequisite for the moral decision making required by the profession. Kohlberg advocated a progressive educational model to facilitate the development of formal operational reasoning required for moral decision making.[27] The success of this model rests on a broad range of experiences, such as experiences in relating to many different people, in different settings, under different circumstances. All these experiences gradually diminish an individual's ethnocentricity and increase respect for and awareness of the larger universe. Again, the relationship between Kohlberg's theory and the focus of social work is most evident. The very thrust of social work, as delineated in the NASW *Code of Ethics,* necessitates a broad social perspective with the common good in the forefront.[28]

Social Work Education in Moral Development

Among the standards for accreditation of educational programs developed by CSWE, two evaluative standards for both the baccalaureate and the master's degrees specifically address the development of moral reasoning: (1) "The program's objectives shall be consistent with the ethics and values of the profession"; and (2) "the program shall make specific, continuous efforts to assure the enrichment of the educational experience it offers by reflecting racial, ethnic, and cultural diversity throughout the curriculum and in all categories of persons related to the program."[29] The first standard emphasizes awareness of professional ethics and values that highlight the need for socially responsible action based on the common good. The second standard demands exposure to and respect for diversity and difference, a prerequisite to ensure the elimination of ethnocentrism. Both are essential for moral reasoning or moral decision making to occur.

An examination of a sample of basic social work textbooks reveals that concern for the first standard—values—together with theory or knowledge, and skills, compose the basis for social work education and ultimately for social work practice.[30] CSWE has provided additional evidence of its ongoing concern about values. In 1959, CSWE supported Muriel Pumphrey's curriculum study on the teaching of values and ethics.[31] Later, it published a collection of manuscripts entitled *Social Work Values in an Age of Discontent.*[32] Throughout the years, CSWE, through its *Journal of Education for Social Work* (now named the *Journal for Social Work Education*), has kept people abreast of major studies dealing with the teaching of values and the incorporation of values among professional social workers.[33] Other studies highlighting the importance of values among professional social workers have been reported regularly in *Social Work.*[34] An entire issue of *Practice Digest* was devoted to the topic "Ethics and Values."[35] NASW also has published a number of important monographs and articles on values.[36] Major publishing houses have provided additional, although somewhat limited, coverage of the topic.[37]

Evidence of the profession's commitment to the latter standard—appreciation of diversity—also is prevalent in the social work literature. The CSWE publication, *The Dual Perspective: Inclusion of Ethnic Minority Content in Social Work Curriculum,* is but one example.[38] Rothman's book and that of Devore and Schlesinger are other outstanding examples.[39] Together, commitment to social work values and an appreciation and respect for diversity provide a solid base for learning moral decision making that is essential for successful professional performance.

Maintaining the Value Base

Although questions have been raised regarding the professional status of social work, the present consensus is that social work does have a unique underlying value base or a moral professional imperative. Because social work is a profession of a variety of actors (some trained and some paraprofessional), there has been ongoing debate, beginning with Abraham Flexner, about its actual status.[40] Flexner thought social work lacked the knowledge base necessary to qualify as a profession, although a value base was certainly in place. Although debate has continued over the years about whether social work qualifies as a profession,[41] this work contends that social work is a profession when professional educational standards are incorporated as a major criterion for membership. It is recognized that professional affiliation/association and the self-selection of people working in the field of social work help to guarantee a certain type/level of value system. It is professional education, however, that specifically serves as a mechanism for the transfer of values and moral decision-making skills to new members entering the profession.

The basic thrust of social work education serves as the key to moral behavior that is representative of the profession. The emphasis of social work education demands a perspective that goes well beyond ethnocentrism to a distinct appreciation of cultural diversity, and it incorporates values that highlight a sense of social responsibility that is focused on ensuring a reasonable minimum standard of living for all members of society. The transmission of values and ethics has been viewed as essential in unifying a widely diversified profession and in giving it identity and meaning.[42] Because of exposure to this content, social workers should differ in their value orientation and behavior from those who have not had similar educational and socialization experiences. Although education is not the only source of influence, the role of education definitely requires additional examination.

Research on Social Work Education

A number of studies have been undertaken on the impact of education on value development. Although some offer minimal evidence of the importance of education in teaching values, others strongly support its significance. Varley's series of studies, for example, showed that graduate education did not foster value consensus among students.[43] She found that personal dimensions—social class, age, and amount of work experience before admission—had a greater impact on value assimilation.[44] On the other hand, Judah presented findings supporting a more positive role for education in value assimilation.[45] She reported that approximately three-fourths of the baccalaureate students in her study showed major levels of value acculturation. Much of that was attributed to classroom and agency experiences and the influence of methodology teachers and agency field instructors. In examining master of social work (MSW) students' attitudes toward public dependency, or toward welfare recipients and the welfare system, Sharwell reported findings more in line with those of Judah; results indicated that values did change from admission to graduation.[46] In their research on student attitudes toward the poor, Grimm and Orten found that age, marital status, SES, undergraduate major, type of educational institution attended, amount of experience before admission, and area of professional specialization were more important than education in determining student attitudes.[47] Cryns also found that gender played a significant role in value acculturation.[48]

Together these researchers raised a series of educational concerns related to the professional socialization process that are addressed here. These concerns are as follows: a need for greater social work value clarification; an examination of the self-selection process in social work; a need for examination of value change related to professional experiences in education and socialization; an examination of the degree of value acculturation and professional socialization in the period immediately after graduation; an additional understanding of the impact of faculty and field instructors on students' professional socialization; an examination of peer influence on value assimilation and professional socialization; and an examination of the influence of personal dimensions on professional value orientation.

Research on Professional Values

Another source of influence on professional socialization and value assimilation and development is professional experience in the field. To determine the impact of experience, some researchers compared students with seasoned practitioners. Costin, for example, compared the students' assessments of their own values with the values professional practitioners thought they should have developed.[49] In examining a random sample of 500 members of the Academy of Certified Social Workers (ACSW), Varley found that, as in her similar studies involving students, demographics played a key role in professional value positions.[50]

Additional studies compared social workers with other professionals. In comparing social work students to business students, Horner, Reid, and Okanes found little difference between the two groups with respect to social insight.[51] Kidneigh and Lundberg compared students in education, engineering, law, library science, nursing, and psychology; they found those in social work more similar to those in education, nursing, and psychology.[52] Social workers tended to come from lower socioeconomic groups and made their career choices later in life. Social workers on the whole tended to be more liberal on those values stressed as important by their profession. In comparing social workers and teachers, McLeod and Meyer found them to differ on six out of nine value dimensions.[53] They suggested the need for additional studies using members of other professional groups.

Some additional concerns emerged and are addressed in this work: How do seasoned professional social workers compare with beginning students and recent practitioners? Do practitioners' professional values change with years of experience? What impact do various personal demographic factors have on professional socialization and value development? How do the values of social work students compare with those of students in other related professions—business, law, psychology, sociology, education, medicine, and nursing? How do undergraduates in the foregoing professions compare with graduates in the same professions? How do the values of various professional groups—business, law, psychology, sociology, education, medicine, and nursing—compare?

Present Societal Values and Social Work

Professional socialization includes assimilation of professional values, ethical imperatives, commitment to rules or the *Code of Ethics,* and development of refined, moral decision-making abilities. Moral decision making involves two critical components: (1) a set of ethical imperatives or rules and (2) the ability to recognize the value of the whole in generating a range of judgments based on the common good. Although professional orientation significantly influences moral decision making, the current tenor of society cannot help but have an impact on the individuals making such decisions. In a fairly detailed treatise on American values and poverty, James stated that two primary values control the perpetuation of policies that maintain poverty in this country: (1) the strong sense of individualism coupled with interest in materialism and (2) hearty ethnocentrism.[54] One can see the effects of such influences in everyday life: the growth of extremist conservative groups, a conservative federal government, and a decrease in growth in governmental support for human services. The conflict is evident between the values identified by James and those identified as essential for professionally responsible action.

In comparing medicine, education, social work, and law, James hypothesized that social work, because of its unique value base, would differ from the other professions in its concern for the poor. Analyses revealed, however, that social workers as a group did not differ. James wrote, "There [was] a distinct line between social workers who [were] trained professionals but [had] little contact with welfare cases, and welfare workers who [handled] the nation's caseload, but [had] rarely been trained professionally" (the latter were more concerned with the elimination of poverty).[55] James identified several factors that she thought distracted workers from attempts to confront the problems of poverty: institutionalism (bureaucratic demands); use of the Freudian model and its emphasis on individualism; lack of professional training in poverty-related issues; heavy emphasis on maintaining professional identity; and workers' mobility up the "ladder" away from welfare positions.[56]

Certainly social workers are confronted with bureaucratic demands. With the vast majority of social workers in direct practice positions, the emphasis on individual client needs may take precedence over social action for the common good. With the excessive curriculum demands on social work education, it is nearly impossible to emphasize poverty-related issues sufficiently. In a world consumed by declassification and competition for limited resources, issues of professional identity frequently are assigned a high priority in the thrust for survival. Last, positions in welfare delivery have tended to be assigned a lower professional status. Those professionals who are more highly educated and capable of sophisticated, moral decision making try rigorously to move to other positions reflecting greater professional status.

One can only hope that the current educational emphasis on cultural diversity has reduced ethnocentrism. The decrease in federal financial support for social work education, however, has resulted in a decrease in student diversity and an increase in middle- and upper-class enrollments, or those less in need of financial assistance. One also can hope that renewed interest in value assimilation and professional socialization will reestablish a strong commitment to and recognition of the basic underlying professional value scheme.

Other researchers in the eighties have attempted to address some of the contributors James recognized as influencing professional values. For example, Austin suggested an action to reduce concern with professional identity issues.[57] He recommended forgetting the Flexner accusation that social work does not qualify as a profession. Flexner dealt us a "narcissistic wound"[58] that has inflicted enough injury and generated more than enough activity. He saw social work as a bona fide profession with a unique perspective that embraces knowledge of cultural diversity and the values and techniques needed for developing a better society. Austin contended it is time for social work to direct attention away from proof of professional status and toward areas that reflect its overall professional mission.

In a similar vein, Loewenberg said that although we social workers need to examine and clarify our knowledge base, the underlying ideology or value base contributes an even more important element to social work.[59] Increased awareness in the area of values is essential for knowledge building, analysis, and effective professional practice. Imre reinforced this concern with values. Historically, social work has attempted to separate knowledge and values. Imre pointed out that both are essential for effective practice.[60]

Reamer also noted the concern with ethics within the social work profession. Social work initially was concerned with the morality of client behavior; since the Settlement House Movement, the focus has shifted to the morality of professional behavior.[61] The current focus is on values considered central to the profession and on ethics or rules that guide professional behavior. In light of current concern with increased knowledge and professional accountability, the thrust has been toward more sophisticated, scientific operationalization of values, moving them beyond a base controlled by intuition toward a more solid one, grounded on research.

It was surprising to note that the 1985 *Report of the Harriet Bartlett Practice Effectiveness Project* did not offer one specific mention of the relationship between values and practice. The $50,000 NASW project supported by funds donated by Harriet Bartlett herself was defined as a

> synthesis of empirical knowledge of practice to be used to improve its quality, to determine policy, and to develop and offer testimony. More significantly, it is the first step in developing for the profession a central and continuing source of information to stimulate research, to expose gaps, and to build the social work knowledge base. This service, when combined with the current computerization of Social Work Abstracts, will constitute a most valuable resource with many potential products.[62]

Of the five major goals of the project, two could be especially relevant to the examination of values and professional morality: (1) "to examine further evaluation studies on social work practice in order to identify factors associated with practice effectiveness; [and] (2) to identify gaps in social work practice research and implications for future research."[63]

Impact of Recent Research on This Project

The lack of a specific mention of values in the Bartlett Project report has provided an incentive for this work. James's findings also demanded reconsideration.[64] It was discouraging to uncover her findings that indicated no difference between social workers and members of related professions in their overall concern for the poor. The work undertaken here also endorsed Loewenberg's contention that values are as essential as knowledge in influencing practice outcomes.[65] This work began to respond to Levy's recent request: "What I would like to propose for the social work agenda for the next fifty years is a focus on valuing with an incidental, though again hardly casual, concern about what must be done about what is valued."[66] To implement this charge, one must be clear about what is valued. Other current researchers support this need for increased understanding of the value base in social work. In presenting models for discharge planning,

Abramson noted the need for incorporating ethical analysis in successful social work practice.[67] She noted models by May, Holmes, and Yezzi, all of whom emphasized the importance of ethics in data collection, the decision-making process, and the selection of possible treatment alternatives.[68] To implement ethical guidelines, one must incorporate and understand the underlying value base. In describing professional action, Reamer noted the need for alternatives to intuition, more technically sophisticated guides for professional behavior, and a more clearly operationalized value base.[69] All the preceding speaks to the need for a greater appreciation of the social work value base. This work was developed in response to these concerns.

General Assumptions

Because values frequently are based on feelings or emotions, they are difficult to examine and measure. This is reflected in the difficulty of locating an appropriate theoretical framework on which to attach value research. In the case of social work, it is especially difficult because of the broad range of professional activities—ranging from individual counseling to the development of social policy, and from income maintenance to legislative lobbying.

In response to the foregoing concerns, this work was founded on the identified need to develop a clearer understanding of social work values as they relate to professional practice in the eighties. It was based on the following five assumptions:

1. Values do determine/influence behavior.
2. A few basic values guide the entirety of social work practice.
3. Social work values are operationalized in a *Code of Ethics* that governs professional attitudes and behavior.
4. A major mission of social work education is the development of moral decision-making abilities based on the distinct social work value base and its ethical correlates.
5. Acculturation to this unique value base contributes to significant differences between social workers and those in other professions with respect to views toward current social issues.

Project Focus

In light of those assumptions, this work was designed to
- develop an instrument with acceptable validity and reliability levels for examining the dimensions underlying sociopolitical values;
- examine the impact of social work education on value assimilation and acculturation;
- determine the influence of self-selection and the admissions process in selecting individuals with a predisposition toward social work values;

■ compare social workers' value orientation with that of other professionals—lawyers, businesspeople, psychologists, nurses, physicians, and educators; and

■ examine the impact of various demographics on basic value orientation. Such demographics include gender, political party affiliation, religion, place of origin, present geographic residence, years of work experience, and marital status.

Notes and References

1. J. Naisbitt, *Megatrends: Ten New Directions Transforming Our Lives* (New York: Warner Books, 1982), p. 131.

2. *For a historical perspective, see* M. Abramovitz, "The Privatization of the Welfare State: A Review," *Social Work,* 31 (July–August 1986), pp. 257–264.

3. G. Gilder, *Wealth and Poverty* (New York: Basic Books, 1981).

4. Proposition 13 was a 1978 California ballot initiative that voters approved by a margin of 65 percent to 35 percent. It cut property tax revenues from $12 billion to $5 billion and reduced government spending accordingly. *For a detailed account, see Facts on File: World News Digest,* 38, No. 1961 (June 9, 1978).

5. *For an overview of modifications in federal spending and support, see* N. Gilbert, "The Welfare State Adrift," *Social Work,* 31 (July–August 1986), pp. 251–256.

6. *For a detailed account, see Facts on File: World News Digest,* 46, No. 2397 (October 31, 1986), p. 815.

7. F. M. Loewenberg, "Professional Ideology, Middle Range Theories, and Knowledge Building for Social Work Practice," *British Journal of Social Work,* 14 (August 1984), pp. 309–322.

8. M. Teicher, "Introduction" in *Values in Social Work: A Re-Examination,* NASW Monograph No. 9 (New York: National Association of Social Workers, Inc., Regional Institute Program, 1967), p. 7.

9. H. M. Bartlett, *The Common Base of Social Work Practice* (New York: National Association of Social Workers, Inc., 1970), p. 63.

10. C. S. Levy, "The Value Base of Social Work," *Journal of Education for Social Work,* 9 (Winter 1973), p. 34.

11. C. Kluckhohn et al., "Values and Value-Orientation in the Theory of Action: An Exploration in Definition and Classification," in T. Parsons and E. Shils, eds., *Toward a General Theory of Action* (Cambridge, Mass.: Harvard University Press, 1951), p. 395.

12. F. Adler, "The Value Concept in Sociology," *American Journal of Sociology,* 62 (1956), pp. 272–279.

13. J. Meddin, "Attitudes, Values and Related Concepts: A System of Classification," *Social Science Quarterly,* 55 (1975), pp. 889–900.

14. F. Kluckhohn and F. Stodbeck, *Variations in Values Orientations* (Evanston, Ill.: Row, Peterson, 1961), pp. 1–2.

15. Meddin, "Attitudes, Values and Related Concepts," p. 892.

16. B. R. Compton and B. Galaway, *Social Work Processes* (3d ed.; Homewood, Ill.: Dorsey Press, 1984), chap. 3, "Values in Social Work," p. 68.

17. W. Schwartz, "The Social Worker in the Group," in National Conference on Social Welfare, ed., *Social Welfare Forum, 1961* (New York: Columbia University Press, 1961), pp. 146–171.

18. F. Loewenberg and R. Dolgoff, *Ethical Decisions for Social Work Practice* (Itasca, Ill.: F. E. Peacock Publishers, 1982), pp. 1–22.

19. H. Lewis, *The Intellectual Base of Social Work Practice: Tools for Thought in a Helping Profession* (New York: The Lois & Samuel Silberman Fund, Haworth Press, 1982), pp. 127–145.

20. Meddin, "Attitudes, Values and Related Concepts," pp. 889–892.

21. *For a discussion of the content of two major works by Emil Durkheim in which he discusses the role of education in moral development*, Moral Education and Education and Society, *see* A. A. Abbott, "Durkheim's Theory of Education: A Case for Mainstreaming," *Peabody Journal of Education*, 58 (July 1981), pp. 235–241.

22. L. Kohlberg, "Early Education: A Cognitive-Developmental View," *Child Development*, 39 (December 1968), pp. 1013–1062; "Stage and Sequence: The Cognitive-Developmental Approach to Socialization," in D. Goslin, ed., *Handbook of Socialization Theory and Research* (New York: Rand McNally, 1969); and L. Kohlberg and R. Mayer, "Development As Aim of Education," *Harvard Educational Review*, 42 (1972), pp. 449–496.

23. T. Lidz, *The Person* (New York: Basic Books, 1968), p. 326.

24. *See* Kohlberg, "Early Education" and J. Piaget, "The Intellectual Development of the Adolescent," in G. Caplan and S. Lebovici, eds., *Adolescence: Psychosocial Perspectives* (New York: Basic Books, 1969).

25. C. Gilligan, *In a Different Voice* (Cambridge, Mass.: Harvard University Press, 1982), p. 18.

26. L. Kohlberg and R. Kramer, "Continuities and Discontinuities in Child and Adult Moral Development," *Human Development*, 12 (1969), pp. 93–120.

27. Kohlberg, "Early Education."

28. *Code of Ethics* (Washington, D.C.: National Association of Social Workers, Inc., 1980).

29. Commission on Accreditation, *Handbook of Accreditation Standards and Procedures* (New York: Council on Social Work Education, 1984), section 1, p. 2; section 2, p. 2; and section 1, standard 12, p. 5; and section 2, standard 13, p. 5.

30. A. Pincus and A. Minahan, *Social Work Practice: Model and Method* (Itasca, Ill.: F.E. Peacock Publishers, 1973); B. R. Compton and B. Galaway,

Social Work Processes (3d ed.; Homewood, Ill.: Dorsey Press, 1984); and M. Siporin, *Introduction to Social Work Practice* (New York: Macmillan Publishing Co., 1975).

31. M. Pumphrey, *The Teaching of Values and Ethics in Social Work Education* (New York: Council on Social Work Education, 1959).

32. K. A. Kendall, ed., *Social Work Values in an Age of Discontent* (New York: Council on Social Work Education, 1970).

33. The following are just a few examples of studies pertaining to values: J. Vigilante, "Between Values and Science: Education for the Profession During a Moral Crisis or Is Proof Truth?" *Journal of Education for Social Work,* 10 (Fall 1974), pp. 107–115; G. R. Sharwell, "Can Values Be Taught? A Study of Two Variables Related to Orientation of Social Work Graduate Students Toward Public Dependency," *Journal of Education for Social Work,* 10 (Spring 1974), pp. 99–105; B. K. Varley, "Social Work Values: Changes in Value Commitments of Students from Admission to MSW Graduation," *Journal of Education for Social Work,* 4 (Fall 1968), pp. 67–76; G. Gross, J. R. Steiner, and L. Rosa, "Educational Doctrines and Social Work Values: Match or Mismatch?" *Journal of Education for Social Work,* 16 (Fall 1980), pp. 21–28; and E. G. Schlesinger, "Graduate Social Work Education: Impact on Social Change and Behavioral Science Orientation," *Journal of Education for Social Work,* 12 (Winter 1976), pp. 113–120.

34. The following are a few examples of research that has been reported in various issues of *Social Work:* C. Pilseker, "Values: A Problem for Everyone," *Social Work,* 23 (January 1978), pp. 54–57; C. S. Levy, "The Context of Social Work Ethics," *Social Work,* 17 (March 1972), pp. 95–101; D. D. Hayes and B. K. Varley, "Impact of Social Work Education on Students' Values," *Social Work,* 10 (July 1965), pp. 40–46; H. Goldstein, "The Neglected Moral Link in Social Work Practice," *Social Work,* 32 (May–June 1987), pp. 181–186; F. G. Reamer, "Ethics Committees in Social Work," *Social Work,* 32 (May–June 1987), pp. 188–192; and B. Z. Cohen, "The Ethics of Social Work Supervision Revisited," *Social Work,* 32 (May–June 1987), pp. 194–196.

35. *Practice Digest,* 6 (Spring 1984), entire issue.

36. Teicher, *Values in Social Work;* A. Keith-Lucas, "Ethics in Social Work," *Encyclopedia of Social Work* (17th ed.; Washington, D.C.: National Association of Social Workers, Inc., 1977), pp. 350–355; H. Bartlett, *The Common Base of Social Work Practice.*

37. Loewenberg and Dolgoff, *Ethical Decision for Social Work Practice;* C. Levy, *Social Work Ethics* (New York: Human Services Press, 1976); and G. Bermant, H. C. Kelman, and D. P. Warwick, eds., *The Ethics of Social Intervention* (New York: John Wiley & Sons, 1978).

38. D. G. Norton et al., *The Dual Perspective: Inclusion of Ethnic Minority Content in the Social Work Curriculum* (New York: Council on Social Work Education, 1978).

39. J. Rothman, ed., *Issues in Race and Ethnic Relations: Theory, Research, and Action* (Itasca, Ill.: F. E. Peacock Publishers, 1977); and W. Devore and E. Schlesinger, *Ethnic-Sensitive Practice* (2d ed., St. Louis, Mo.: C. V. Mosby Co., 1987).

40. A. Flexner, "Is Social Work a Profession?" *Proceedings of the National Conference of Charities and Correction* (Chicago: Hildman Printing Co., 1915).

41. M. Rein, "Social Work in Search of a Radical Profession," *Social Work,* 15 (April 1970), pp. 13-28; and H. Specht, "The Deprofessionalization of Social Work," *Social Work,* 17 (March 1972), pp. 3-15.

42. D. N. Noble and J. E. King, "Values: Passing on the Torch Without Burning the Runner," *Social Casework,* 62 (December 1981), pp. 579-584.

43. B. K. Varley, "Social Work Values: Changes in Value Commitments of Students from Admission to MSW Graduation," *Journal of Education for Social Work,* 14 (Fall 1968), pp. 67-76.

44. B. K. Varley, "Socialization in Social Work Education," *Social Work,* 8 (July 1963), pp. 102-109.

45. E. H. Judah, "Acculturation to the Social Work Profession in Baccalaureate Social Work Education," *Journal of Education for Social Work,* 12 (Fall 1976), pp. 65-71.

46. G. R. Sharwell, "Can Values Be Taught? A Study of Two Variables Related to Orientation of Social Work Graduate Students Toward Public Dependency," *Journal of Education for Social Work,* 10 (Spring 1974), pp. 99-105.

47. J. W. Grimm and J. D. Orten, "Student Attitudes Toward the Poor," *Social Work,* 18 (January 1973), pp. 94-100.

48. A. G. Cryns, "Social Work Education and Student Ideology: A Multivariate Study of Professional Socialization," *Journal of Education for Social Work,* 13 (Winter 1977), pp. 44-51.

49. L. Costin, "Values in Social Work Education: A Study," *Social Service Review,* 38 (September 1964), pp. 271-280.

50. B. K. Varley, "Are Social Workers Dedicated to Service?" *Social Work,* 11 (April 1966), pp. 84-91.

51. W. Horner, P. N. Reid, and M. Okanes, "Manipulative Orientation and Social Insight: A Comparative Study of Social Work and Business Administration Students," *Journal of Education for Social Work,* 14 (Fall 1978), pp. 56-63.

52. J. C. Kidneigh and H. W. Lundberg, "Are Social Work Students Different?" *Social Work,* 3 (July 1958), pp. 57-61.

53. D. L. McLeod and H. J. Meyer, "A Study of the Values of Social Workers," in E. J. Thomas, ed., *Behavioral Science for Social Workers* (New York: Free Press, 1967), pp. 401-416.

54. D. B. James, *Poverty, Politics, and Change* (Englewood Cliffs, N.J.: Prentice-Hall, 1972).

55. Ibid., p. 95.
56. Ibid.
57. M. Austin, "The Flexner Myth and the History of Social Work," *Social Service Review,* 57 (September 1983), pp. 357-377.
58. This is a psychoanalytic term that arose in a discussion of Austin's comments with B. L. Davis, ACSW, adjunct professor of social work, Rutgers University, Camden, N.J.
59. Loewenberg, "Professional Ideology, Middle Range Theories, and Knowledge Building for Social Work Practice," p. 320.
60. R. W. Imre, "The Nature of Knowledge in Social Work," *Social Work,* 29 (January-February 1984), pp. 41-45.
61. F. G. Reamer, "Ethical Content in Social Work," *Social Casework,* 61 (November 1980), pp. 531-540.
62. L. Videka-Sherman, *Harriet M. Bartlett Practice Effectiveness Project* (Silver Spring, Md.: National Association of Social Workers, Inc., 1985), p. 1.
63. Ibid., p. 3.
64. James, *Poverty, Politics, and Change.*
65. Loewenberg, "Professional Ideology, Middle Range Theories, and Knowledge Building for Social Work Practice."
66. C. S. Levy, "Values and Ethics: Foundations of Social Work," in S. Dillick, ed., *Value Foundations of Social Work: Ethical Basis for a Human Service Profession* (Detroit, Mich.: Wayne State University, 1984), pp. 17-29.
67. M. Abramson, "A Model for Organizing an Ethical Analysis of the Discharge Planning Process," *Social Work in Health Care,* 9 (Fall 1983), pp. 45-52.
68. W. May, "Professional Ethics: Setting, Terrain, and Teacher," in D. Callahan and S. Bok, eds., *Ethics Teaching in Higher Education* (New York: Plenum Press, 1980), pp. 205-241; C. Holmes, "Bioethical Decision Making: An Approach to Improve the Process," *Medical Care,* 17 (1979), pp. 1131-1138; and R. Yezzi, *Medical Ethics* (New York: Holt, Rinehart, & Winston, 1980).
69. F. G. Reamer, Conflicts in Professional Duty in Social Work," *Social Casework,* 63 (December 1982), pp. 579-585.

T · W · O

Professional Opinion Scale:
Determining Professional Socialization in Light of Value Orientation

♦

The study of values in large numbers of individuals required a reliable and easily administered measuring instrument. This chapter contains an overview of the development of the Professional Opinion Scale (POS) and a discussion of the scale's key components. A copy of the scale and a detailed accounting of its development appear in appendixes A and B.

Studies of Social Work Values Using Social Psychology Scales

Although much has been written about values, only a few social workers have conducted empirical research on values in the past 25 years. Of those, the majority used existing data collection instruments developed primarily by social psychologists. The *College Vocabulary Test,* the *Authoritarian Personality Social Attitudes Battery,* and the *Hollingshead Two-Factor Index of Social Position*[1] were used in a classic study by Kidneigh and Lundberg designed to determine whether the values of social work students differed from those of students in engineering, education, law, library science, nursing, and psychology.[2] Twenty additional questions were included to gather specific demographic information about the students. In another classic study, Costin determined the opinions of social workers about the following six specific personal interests (values): (1) theoretic, (2) economic, (3) aesthetic, (4) social, (5) political, and (6) religious.[3] She used the *Study of Values Scale.*[4]

Grimm and Orten examined social work attitudes toward the poor using a 40-item scale developed by Peterson, which in turn was based on the scale format used by Hovland and Sherif involving an 11-point Likert-type scale.[5] Sharwell used a 16-item Likert-type scale developed by Anderson to measure the attitudes of social work students toward poverty, racism, and mental health.[6] Cryns examined the relationship between the educational status of social work students and their professional ideological orientation.[7] He used the *Wrightsman Philosophy of Human Nature Scale,* a Likert-type scale designed to assess a person's expectations about human nature; the *Feagin Poverty Scale,* 11 statements designed to assess general beliefs about the causes of poverty[8]; and the *Economic Success Scale,* a variation of the Feagin scale developed specifically for the study.

Studies of Social Work Values Using Scales Developed Within the Profession

Varley was one of the first to develop an instrument designed specifically to measure social work values—the *Social Work Questionnaire.*[9] The scale includes four subscales designed to assess the following values: commitment to equal rights, dedication to service to others, psychological-mindedness, and universalism, or the ability to overcome personal needs in favor of professional responsibility. She used the *Social Work Questionnaire* to compare beginning social work students with recent graduates. In later studies she used the instrument to examine the value orientation of members of ACSW[10] and changes in students' value commitments from the time of admission to the time of graduation.[11] Judah employed Varley's *Social Work Questionnaire* in a later study designed to compare the value orientation of bachelor of social work (BSW) students, MSW students, and social work faculty.[12]

McLeod and Meyer abstracted 10 major value dimensions from social work classics to develop their value scale (the first dimension listed in each item is the preferred one): (1) individual worth versus system goals; (2) personal liberty versus societal control; (3) group responsibility versus individual responsibility; (4) security-satisfaction versus struggle, suffering, and denial; (5) relativism–pragmatism versus absolutism–sacredness; (6) innovative change versus traditionalism; (7) diversity versus homogeneity; (8) cultural determinism versus inherent human nature; (9) interdependence versus individual autonomy; and (10) individualization versus stereotyping.[13] One hundred attitude statements (10 for each category) were selected from several hundred on the basis of judgments by a panel of social work educators and social researchers.

From a methodological perspective, the social work value scale developed by Howard and Flaitz is the most significant to date.[14] Howard and

Flaitz refer to their scale as one designed to measure "socioprofessional ideology," a term coined by Cryns to describe a positive orientation to issues considered of primary concern to social workers.[15] The four values their scale was designed to measure are (1) social justice, (2) individual freedom, (3) human nature, and (4) human rights.

Methodological shortcomings were noted in relation to each scale. This is not surprising because all the scales represented beginning attempts at developing an instrument that could measure degree of concurrence with basic social work values. These early attempts were considered crucial in development of POS, and the methodological improvements suggested by each were incorporated into construction of POS.

Rationale for Development of POS

In light of the research discussed, POS was developed to collect data for the continued examination of the underlying ideology or value base of social work. It was assumed that the value base of any profession should be evident in the code of ethics of the major professional organization and in its public policy or position papers. A second assumption, based on the value, attitude, and opinion hierarchy delineated by Meddin[16] and described in chapter 1, recognizes that opinions and behavior directly reflect one's underlying value base.

If you and I were sitting in a circle of people on the prairie, and if I were then to place a painted drum or an eagle feather in the middle of this circle, each of us would perceive these objects differently. Our vision of them would vary according to our individual positions in the circle.... Every single one of our previous experiences in life will affect in some way the mental perspective from which we see the world around us.
—"Hyemeyohsts Storm," *Seven Arrows*
(New York: Ballantine Books, 1972), p. 4.

NASW—the major professional organization for social workers—has both a code of ethics and a wide variety of public social policy statements, which were developed by its members. The *Code of Ethics* specifically delineates preferred professional behavior.[17] The Public Social Policy Statements illustrate the impact of both the value base and the derived ethical principles.[18] One of these statements is that a social worker should advocate changes in policy and legislation to improve social conditions and promote social justice. Because of the breadth and timeliness of these opinion papers, they were selected as the source of statements composing POS. In addition, because NASW members developed the statements, it is believed that the influence of the underlying value base and the derived *Code of Ethics* should be evident in the statements themselves.

NASW Public Social Policy Statements

The NASW Public Social Policy Statements (developmental details of which are presented in appendix A) reflect the spectrum of topics about which NASW members express major concern (Table 1). Topics such as recreational services, the handicapped, and family planning reflect ongoing interests. Homelessness, acquired immune deficiency syndrome (AIDS), and parental kidnapping reflect NASW's sense of current issues. The 41 topics clearly illustrate the range of issues concerning social workers. With each delegate assembly (the national forum for finalizing policies), new policies are introduced, as well as revisions of earlier ones (for example, the 1981 housing policy was replaced with a 1984 revision, as was the 1979 health policy).

Policy statements do not include recommendations for NASW implementation; rather, they state broadly what the response of NASW members to the overall problem area should be and what NASW's position should be in relation to specific components of the problem. For example, in relation to AIDS, the policy "urged comprehensive research, public education, educational and social support for victims, and protection of their civil rights."

Development of POS Items from the Public Social Policy Statements

Items for POS, a 5-point Likert-type scale, were developed to reflect the content of the entire set of NASW Public Social Policy Statements. The details surrounding the development of POS are presented in appendix A; a copy of the scale is presented as appendix B. The final version of POS includes 121 items based on the NASW Public Social Policy Statements and 26 items designed to collect pertinent demographic information.

Pilot Testing of POS

Initially, POS was administered to pilot samples of 203, 155, and 150 (details are supplied in appendix A). The intent of the selection of these pilot groups was to assure comparable samples, each reflecting wide variability; that goal was achieved. Respondents included BSW and MSW students and graduates, social work faculty and field instructors, social service agency staff members, and students in business. More than 50 percent in all three samples were between ages 26 and 45, and 25 percent were male. More

Table 1.
Public Policy Statements of NASW: Topic and Date

Topic	Date of Most Recent Statement
Abortion	1975
AIDS	1984
Adolescent pregnancy	1984
Adoption and foster care	1979
Alcoholism and alcohol-related problems	1979
Alternative work patterns	1981
Children and youth	1975
Civil liberties and justice	1971
Community development	1981
Corporal punishment of children in schools and custodial settings	1984
Deinstitutionalization	1977
Domestic violence	1979
Education	1979
Energy	1981
Family planning	1967
Family policy	1981
Gay issues	1977
General revenue sharing and block grants	1984
Handicapped persons: rehabilitation	1967
Handicapped persons: rights and needs	1977
Health	1984
Homelessness	1984
Hospice care	1981
Housing	1984
Immigration	1979
Income allocations and guarantees	1975
Information utilization and confidentiality	1975
International policy on human rights	1981
Juvenile delinquency and adult crime	1977
Long-term care	1979
Parental kidnapping	1984
Peace and social welfare	1977
Racism	1979
Recreational services	1967
Social services	1975
Social work in rural areas	1981
Status offenders	1979
Substance abuse	1975
Tax reform	1975
Volunteers and social service systems	1977
Women's issues	1977

SOURCES: *Compilation of Public Social Policy Statements* (Silver Spring, Md.: National Association of Social Workers, Inc., September 1983); and *NASW Delegate Assembly Handbook* (Silver Spring, Md.: National Association of Social Workers, Inc., September 1984).

than 80 percent were white, with slightly less than half the remainder being black. Slightly fewer than 50 percent were married, and more than 50 percent were childless. Just over 50 percent were registered Democrats, 15 percent were registered Republicans, and 25 percent expressed no political party affiliation. One-third viewed themselves as politically liberal, one-half as moderate. Slightly fewer than one-third were Roman Catholic and another third Protestant. More than three-fourths reported a family income of at least $20,000 and well over one-fifth reported income of more than $45,000. More than 90 percent held a bachelor's degree and more than 33 percent a master's degree. Nearly 50 percent had fewer than six years of professional experience, and about 25 percent reported 10 or more years of experience.

Initial Identification of POS Value Subscales

The responses of sample 1 to the entire 121 items comprising POS were analyzed using principal components factor analysis to identify major value dimensions within the scale.[19] A description of criteria for analysis is included in appendix A. Use of the two additional pilot samples reinforced the four values identified in sample 1, thus reaffirming the reliability of these basic dimensions (see appendix A for a description of the replications). Judgments by a panel of experts support the validity of the identified values. Additional analyses (analyses of variances [ANOVAs] and comparisons of group means are reported in appendix A) illustrate the ability of POS to differentiate among various populations (for example, social work students, social service agency personnel, and businesspeople).

Identified Value Dimensions

The four major value dimensions identified were (1) respect for basic rights, (2) sense of social responsibility, (3) commitment to individual freedom, and (4) support of self-determination. A list of items composing each value dimension is included in appendix A.

The values as identified appear to support a hierarchy emphasizing moral decision making in our society. Basically, the focus of our national philosophy is respect for basic rights: life, liberty, and the pursuit of happiness (value 1). With commitment to basic rights comes the sense of social responsibility (value 2) to guarantee a certain standard of living for all citizens. Thus, such government programs as Old-Age, Survivors, and Disability Insurance (commonly referred to as social security); Aid to Families with Dependent Children; Supplemental Security Income; Medicare; Medicaid; and unemployment compensation are designed to guarantee a certain standard of living. Although our nation has made a commitment to the preceding, ideas about implementation and eligibility requirements vary. The ongoing impact of the Protestant ethic and the influence of social Darwinism, to say nothing of the ever-present effects of Horatio Alger, influence how these programs are implemented. Thus, the commitment to individual freedom (value 3) versus social control varies with the current interpretation of freedom. Upon approaching the last value dimension in the hierarchy, support of self-determination (value 4), or individual decision making, the impact of current philosophy becomes even more evident.

For example, the top of the hierarchy—basic rights—has continued to be advocated throughout time. The vast majority of U.S. citizens agree that these rights are essential to our basic national philosophy and existence. The second value—a sense of social responsibility—varies with the current interpretation, which is influenced strongly by national views on matters such as a balanced national budget and government preferences for providing "guns or butter." It is also arguable that one's sense of social responsibility varies with one's degree of personal comfort and/or one's moral decision-making abilities. According to Kohlberg, and as delineated in chapter 1, if one has truly mastered moral decision making, one goes beyond self to incorporate the greater social whole.[20] Ability to incorporate that larger perspective undoubtedly is linked to personal difficulties, strength, suffering, and peer pressure, as well as to the influence of basic competing philosophies, such as "survival of the fittest" or the Protestant ethic.

Commitment to individual freedom is even more sensitive to the interpretations of those developing the pertinent laws and programs, including eligibility requirements. If one believes that strong social control improves individual functioning, then a tighter rein is enforced; if one believes the opposite, increased avenues for individual decision making are developed. With the rise of extremist conservative groups, such as the Moral Majority and Phyllis Schlafly's Eagle Forum, greater restriction or control is being placed on individual choice in such areas as birth control, family planning, workfare, and abortion. During the sixties and seventies, before the conservative upsurge, greater emphasis was placed on individual choice in these areas. This is evidenced by the increase in family planning programs during that period, the Supreme Court ruling (January 1973) overruling state laws that prohibited or restricted a woman's right to abortion during the first trimester, and the inclusion of birth control information in most high school health curricula.

The fourth value—support of self-determination—encourages the exercise of individual decision-making, not only by offering freedom of choice but by setting up opportunities to develop and exercise that freedom.

It is the author's contention that most U.S. citizens have a strong commitment to the first value—respect for basic rights. This is the fiber of society, highlighted throughout our country and reinforced by our educational system. Those with more developed, moral decision-making abilities should score higher on sense of social responsibility than those with less developed, moral decision-making abilities. While number of years of formal education does not guarantee mastery of moral decision making, it should influence this ability positively, especially if one of the basic goals of the individual's education has been to develop a sense of social responsibility.

Commitment to individual freedom implies respect for others, their needs, and their personal decision-making abilities. It represents a respect for diversity and individual preference. This does not entail overriding the common good but rather accepting individual interpretation within the confines of the group. Support of self-determination encourages individuals to exercise their individual preferences and decision-making abilities. Again the presence of both these values should vary, depending on educational experience and professional orientation, as well as on basic demographic characteristics, such as religious orientation and educational level of the family of origin.

The present factor analysis provides an empirical base for the CSWE curriculum policy statements for baccalaureate and master of social work programs.[21] The four identified dimensions reflect the essential social work values outlined in the policy statements. The first dimension—respect for basic rights—reflects the primary value: "Social workers hold that people should have equal access to resources, services, and opportunities for the accomplishment of life tasks, the alleviation of distress, and the realization of their aspirations and values [statement 5.1]." The second dimension—sense of social responsibility—reflects the content of one of the five secondary value statements or practice principles derived from the primary value already stated. "Social workers contribute to making social institutions more humane and responsive to human needs [statement 5.2.3]." The third dimension—commitment to individual freedom—reflects the content of an additional value statement or practice principle: "Social workers demonstrate respect for and acceptance of the unique characteristics of diverse populations [statement 5.2.4]." The fourth dimension—support of self-determination—reflects the content of two additional value statements or practice principles: (1) "Social workers' professional relationships are built on their regard for individual worth and human dignity and are furthered by mutual participation, acceptance, confidentiality, honesty, and responsible handling of conflict [statement 5.2.1]"; and (2) "Social workers respect people's right to choose, to contract for services, and to participate in the helping process [statement 5.2.2]."

The four identified values also strongly reflect the content of the NASW *Code of Ethics*.[22] SECTION VI of the code, entitled "The Social Worker's Ethical Responsibility to Society," highlights practice based on respect for basic rights (SECTION VI, PARTS 1 and 2) as well as a strong sense of social responsibility (SECTION VI, PARTS 6 and 7). SECTION VI also emphasizes commitment to individual freedom (PARTS 3 and 4). SECTION II, PART G, demands effort by social workers to foster maximum self-determination in clients.

Major Expectation

Based on the content of POS, social workers should receive higher total value scores than members of other professions. This should be increasingly true as one progresses from value 1 (respect for basic values) to value 4 (support of self-determination). Seasoned social work practitioners should score higher than recent graduates and recent graduates higher than beginning students. Social work faculty and social service agency personnel with similar educational and professional experiences should receive comparable scores.

Although the generation of dimensions or factors using principal components factor analysis is based on procedures with no regard for content or meaning, the four value dimensions identified in POS do appear to contain related items that support value dimensions delineated in the social work literature. The use of two replications (sample 2 and sample 3) offers strong reinforcement for the value dimensions identified in the initial factoring of sample 1. The rankings of three independent judges, as described in appendix A, also support the identified values. Additional analyses (analyses of covariance and Tukey's comparisons of group means) illustrate the ability of POS to identify differences and to differentiate between groups holding dissimilar value orientations.

In summary, because of its reliability, validity, and ability to differentiate, POS was determined to be a suitable instrument for measuring respondents' opinions about current public social issues and for determining their degree of concurrence with basic, underlying social work values. Because of its format, which lends itself to computer scoring, POS was deemed a sufficiently convenient scale for use with large samples of people.

Notes and References

1. J. C. Kidneigh and H. C. Lundberg, "Are Social Work Students Different?" *Social Work*, 3 (July 1958), pp. 57–61.

2. H. G. Gough and H. Sampson, *The College Vocabulary Test* (Berkeley: University of California Press, 1954); T. W. Adorno et al., *The Authoritarian Personality* (New York: Harper & Brothers, 1950); and A. B. Hollingshead, R. Ellis, and E. Kirby, "Social Mobility and Mental Illness," *American Sociological Review*, 19 (October 1954), pp. 579–582.

3. L. B. Costin, "Values in Social Work Education: A Study," *Social Service Review*, 38 (September 1964), pp. 271–280.

4. G. W. Allport, P. E. Vernon, and G. Lindzey, *Study of Values: A Scale for Measuring the Dominant Interests in Personality* (New York: Houghton Mifflin Co., 1951).

5. J. W. Grimm and J. D. Orten, "Student Attitudes Toward the Poor," *Social Work*, 18 (January 1973), pp. 94-100; J. H. Peterson, "A Disguised Structured Instrument for the Assessment of Attitudes Toward the Poor." Unpublished PhD dissertation, University of Oklahoma, Norman, 1967; C. I. Hovland and M. Sherif, "Judgmental Phenomena and Scales of Attitude Measurement: Item Displacement in Thurstone Scales," *Journal of Abnormal and Social Psychology*, 47 (October 1952), pp. 822-832; and M. Sherif and C. I. Hovland, "Judgmental Phenomena and Scales of Attitude Measurement: Placement of Items with Individual Choice of Number Categories," *Journal of Abnormal and Social Psychology*, 48 (January 1953), pp. 135-141.

6. G. R. Sharwell, "Can Values Be Taught? A Study of Two Variables Related to Orientation of Social Work Graduate Students Toward Public Dependency," *Journal of Education for Social Work*, 10 (Spring 1974), pp. 99-105; C. L. Anderson, "Development of an Objective Measure of Orientation Toward Public Dependency," *Social Forces*, 44 (September 1965), pp. 107-113; and C. L. Anderson, "A Preliminary Study of Generational Economic Dependency Orientations," *Social Forces*, 45 (June 1967), pp. 16-20.

7. A. G. Cryns, "Social Work Education and Student Ideology: A Multivariate Study of Professional Socialization," *Journal of Education for Social Work*, 13 (Winter 1977), pp. 44-51.

8. L. Wrightsman, "Measurement of Philosophies of Human Nature," *Psychological Reports*, 14 (1964), pp. 743-751; and J. Feagin, "Poverty: We Still Believe That God Helps Those Who Help Themselves," *Psychology Today*, 6 (1972), pp. 101-110, 129.

9. B. K. Varley, "Socialization in Social Work Education," *Social Work*, 8 (July 1963), pp. 102-109.

10. B. K. Varley, "Are Social Workers Dedicated to Service?" *Social Work*, 11 (April 1966), pp. 84-91.

11. B. K. Varley, "Social Work Values: Changes in Value Commitments of Students from Admission to MSW Graduation," *Journal of Education for Social Work*, 4 (Fall 1968), pp. 67-76.

12. E. H. Judah, "Values: The Uncertain Component in Social Work," *Journal of Education for Social Work*, 15 (Spring 1979), pp. 79-86.

13. D. L. McLeod and H. J. Meyer, "Chapter 30: A Study of the Values of Social Workers," in E. J. Thomas, ed., *Behavioral Science for Social Workers* (New York: Free Press, 1967), pp. 401-416.

14. T. U. Howard and J. Flaitz, "A Scale to Measure the Humanistic Attitudes of Social Work Students," *Social Work Research and Abstracts*, 18 (Winter 1982), pp. 11-18.

15. Cryns, "Social Work Education and Student Ideology," p. 44.

16. J. Meddin, "Attitudes, Values and Related Concepts: A System of Classification," *Social Science Quarterly*, 55 (1975), pp. 889-900.

17. *Code of Ethics* (New York: National Association of Social Workers, Inc., adopted 1979, effective July 1, 1980).

18. *Compilation of Public Social Policy Statements* (Silver Spring, Md.: National Association of Social Workers, Inc., 1983).

19. Data were analyzed using the *Statistical Package for the Social Sciences,* expanded version *(SPSS-X),* as described in *SPSS-X* (2d ed.; Chicago: SPSS, 1986); see chap. 37, "Factor," pp. 714–730. Additional information on factor analysis is presented in earlier versions of the SPSS user's guides. See references in appendix A.

20. L. Kohlberg, "Development of Moral Character and Moral Ideology," in M. Hoffman and L. Hoffman, eds., *Review of Child Development Research* (New York: Russell Sage Foundation, 1964).

21. CSWE Commission on Accreditation, Appendix I, "Curriculum Policy for the Master's Degree and Baccalaureate Degree Programs in Social Work Education," in *Handbook of Accreditation Standards and Procedures* (New York: Council on Social Work Education, 1984).

22. *Code of Ethics* (New York: National Association of Social Workers, Inc., 1980).

T·H·R·E·E

Choice:
The Selection of a Profession

◆

Professional socialization has been defined as that process by which individuals are influenced or molded to assimilate and reflect the value dimensions of a given profession. To understand the impact of the educational process as well as that of professional work experience, one must appreciate the degree of socialization that is present before that experience, or a baseline measure. The fact that one selects a given profession may depend on a number of factors, such as intelligence or family pressure. It may also be that one is predisposed to the values and perspectives endorsed by the particular profession.

In her study of beginning MSW students, Barnard found that the majority of her sample ($n = 22$) exhibited evidence of significant positive assimilation of three out of five basic social work values—self-awareness, growth or change, and humanism.[1] She defined *self-awareness* as being in touch with one's own feelings versus a self-protective orientation. She described *growth/change* as reflecting the extent to which one is willing to change or to resist change in both social and personal arenas and *humanism* as a preference for a person versus task orientation. Evidence was minimal of the presence of the remaining two values—*social relations,* referring to an egalitarian mode versus an authoritarian one, and *personal/social,* referring to how well one is able to incorporate both internal and external dimensions of a situation versus an "either–or" orientation. Barnard stressed the need for baseline measurement of both these values, especially in relation to the student selection and admission process. She believed that these latter two values historically had been held in less esteem by the profession and, therefore, may not have been as essential in the admissions process. This would explain why their prevalence in the sixties, when her study was conducted, was of little concern.

Social relations and personal/social values have been given greater significance in two documents of the eighties held to be of primary importance by the social work profession: the CSWE curriculum policy statement and the NASW *Code of Ethics*.[2] The current project focuses on examining their role and identifying their presence. This current emphasis, including egalitarianism, respect for diversity and self-determination, the need for social justice, and the role of social responsibility, is undoubtedly a reflection of the times. The sixties produced an external generation, most of whom supported efforts highlighting the preceding value dimensions. It was a time when universal rights were paramount and social responsibility the cry of the day. The civil rights movement, the war on poverty, and the concept of "maximum feasible participation" all could be construed as evidence of that support. The eighties, on the other hand, is a time of the "me" generation, when having the "right" car is, for many people, far more important than the concept of "a car in every garage," or adequate transportation for everyone. The guarantee of individual rights stressed in the sixties has been replaced by the guarantee of individualism, a concept whose presence has ebbed and flowed with the times.[3]

Historically, social work values have not been independent of current societal values; rather, they have been represented as an extension of those basic values. Because social work receives its sanction from society, its values must be somewhat compatible with the general values espoused by that society. It is important to note, however, that social work's values historically have *not* been identical with those of the larger society. In some cases, social work has by its very nature pushed a less popular position, forcing an expansion of society's vision. Vigilante, in fact, earmarked social work as the conscience of the community.[4] Others, on the other hand, have characterized social work as both "liberal" and "conservative"—"conservative" because it encourages change through "legal, official, bureaucratic, and socially approved means" and "liberal" because of its sense of social responsibility and its "commitment to relieve human suffering."[5]

Although Taber and Vattano perceive conservatism and liberalism as being in competition,[6] Koeske and Crouse argue that the two are manifestations of the same basic underlying values, the balance of which depends on the prevailing social values.[7] When social values are more liberal, more liberal social work values are tolerated; when social values are more conservative, social work intervention is forced to be more conservative. The mission of the profession, however, remains the same.

Current times are marked by society's conservative bent, the rise of the Yuppie generation, the growth of the Moral Majority, and a return to or a reaffirmation of the "survival of the fittest" perspective. Thus, social work is being forced to restate its interest in protecting and ensuring the rights of individuals and in guaranteeing the satisfaction of their basic human needs. Thus, emphasis on social responsibility and the protection of individual differences is increased. Emphasis is on the continued development, adherence to, and advocacy of the NASW Public Social Policy Statements and the underlying professional value base reflected in those statements also is increased.

Current Focus on Individualism

Individualism has been emphasized to various degrees throughout American history. During early developmental stages, Alexis de Tocqueville noted its influence in describing American democracy. He also noted with trepidation the possible isolation such a philosophical orientation might promote. Bellah and his colleagues expand on this theme, illustrating how Tocqueville's anticipations may have become realities today. The title of their observations, *Habits of the Heart*, was that phraseology used by Tocqueville himself in describing American mores.[8] The analysis of interviews conducted by Bellah et al. between 1979 and 1984 with more than 200 Americans reveals three main variations on the theme of individualism: (1) success or moving up the corporate ladder (survival of the fittest); (2) freedom or being left alone by others; and (3) justice or equal opportunities for everyone to pursue whatever he or she understands as happiness. Significantly, all three variations reflect a sense of being left alone; none reflects an affirmative action stance or the socially responsible, facilitative action necessary to convert all three variations into universal options. Thus, the primary "habit of the heart" appears to be a focus on self-satisfaction, a stance based on individualism.

Bellah and fellow researchers offer a historical account of this current resurgence of individualism.[9] Their notions are highly compatible with those offered by economists and social welfare historians. From the beginning of the late nineteenth century until after World War I, the two primary forces operating in society were the "establishment" and "populism." The establishment represented a paternalistic stance based on the Protestant ethic and a strong sense of "noblesse oblige" and populism, a governmental commitment to monitoring economic life for the well-being of its citizens. Both forces tried to incorporate industrial society under a scheme designed to promote public moral order. Neither emphasized major government involvement. The Great Depression brought both forces to the shocking realization that their laissez faire approach was inadequate. From this chaos emerged another pair of forces: "welfare liberalism" and "neocapitalism." Welfare liberalism demanded a much more active role for the government, with the development of the New Deal and, later, the Great Society programs. Its counterpart, neocapitalism, with its roots in early paternalism, stressed the importance of private ventures versus public expenditures. As the economic difficulties of the seventies began to emerge, the governmental purse strings grew tighter and the time was ripe for a return to the individualism and reduced government spending emphasized by neocapitalism. It was on this platform that Ronald Reagan developed his popularity.

The relationship between the economy and the rise of individualism and its impact on American values is aptly summarized in *Habits of the Heart:*

> When times are prosperous, we do not mind a modest increase in welfare. When times are not so prosperous, we think that at least our own successful careers will save us and our families from failure and despair. We are attracted, against our skepticism, to the idea that poverty will be alleviated by the crumbs that fall from the rich man's table, as the Neocapitalist ideology tells us. Some of us often feel, and most of us sometimes feel, that we are only someone if we have "made it" and can look down on those who have not. The American dream is often a very private dream of being the star, the uniquely successful and admirable one, the one who stands out from the crowd of ordinary folk who don't know how. And since we have believed in that dream for a long time and worked very hard to make it come true, it is hard for us to give it up, even though it contradicts another dream that we have—that of living in a society that would really be worth living in.
>
> What we fear above all, and what keeps the new world powerless to be borne, is that if we give up our dream of private success for a more genuinely integrated societal community, we will be abandoning our separation and individuation, collapsing into dependence and tyranny. What we find hard to see is that it is the extreme fragmentation of the modern world that really threatens our individuation; that what is best in our separation and individuation, our sense of dignity and autonomy as persons, requires a new integration if it is to be sustained.[10]

Based on the foregoing, one can see evidence of the strong roots of individualism. The authors' research supports the findings of James, who, even at the height of the war on poverty, noted the strong presence of materialism, individualism, and ethnocentrism in our society and its impact on poverty.[11] In good times, society is reluctant to share; as the economy tightens, the urge to share is greatly diminished and the need to emphasize individualism and survival of the fittest, enhanced. Accompanying the rise of individualism is the increased importance of one's family, one's church, one's community—all dimensions strongly related to individual, personal well-being.

With the preceding as a representation of current societal values, several questions emerge: "Are social workers different?" Are they controlled by the current societal stance? In the immediate case, are students who select social work as a profession significantly different from those who choose to enter other professions? More specifically, do students who select social work transcend societal values by exhibiting evidence of greater concurrence with the value base espoused by that profession?

Social Work Perspective

The preceding questions have been examined by a number of researchers. In answering the question "Are social work students different?" Kidneigh and Lundberg found that in comparison with students in law, education, nursing, psychology, engineering, and library science, social work students were more liberal on antidemocratic tendencies, ethnocentrism, political-economic conservatism, and the interpretation of traditional family ideology.[12] They determined that social work represented a "unique" pool, that social work students were not selected from the common pool from which students for the other professions were selected.

In their study of social work values over time, Koeske and Crouse found that the values of social workers did in fact change to reflect the changes in the larger society.[13] Using the *Rokeach Value Survey* and the *Wilson-Patterson Conservatism Scale* to measure values, they found their 1979–80 sample of social workers to be significantly more conservative than their 1975 sample. Importantly, social workers, as a group, remained more liberal over time than Rokeach's general samples when age, income, or education were controlled. Interestingly, social workers did not rank equality as more important than any comparison samples, and they ranked freedom as less important than all comparison samples.

Occupation can be a calling....There is both an outward and an inward significance to the idea. The outward is the larger context within which any person's contributions can be seen to have significance....The inward significance is twofold: there is a dignity to one's work...and there is a sense of fulfillment and meaning that can come from being of service to others and to the common good.
—J. M. Gustafson, "Professions as 'Callings,'" *Social Service Review*, 56 (1982), p. 504.

If social workers are in fact different, at what point in the professional socialization process do these differences become notable? In describing how individuals select a profession, Gustafson refers to a moral calling akin to what John Calvin referred to as a "secret calling" in speaking of the religious.[14] This, he states, is true especially of relatively low-salaried professions designed to serve human needs. His theory suggests that social workers have a propensity for the field that influences their selection of that profession. Hayes and Varley refer to this early assimilation of values as an "anticipatory socialization process" or "the taking on of values of a group to which one aspires to belong."[15] They found that women, in general, exhibited greater assimilation of social work values than did men. Women in social work did not differ significantly, however, from the general population of college women. Men in social work did differ significantly from their non-social work counterparts.

Their findings are similar to those reported by Kidneigh and Lundberg, who also noted that female social work students did not vary greatly from other college females.[16] Males, on the other hand, demonstrated greater deviance from the general male norm. Thus, they also concluded that males who enter social work are required to engage in greater anticipatory socialization. Group comparisons reveal that values of social work students, males and females collectively, did differ from those of the general college population.

Sharwell also found that social work students differed significantly from the general population in their attitudes toward public dependency.[17] In this vein, Cryns found the values of social work students to differ from those of students from other disciplines; those of undergraduate and graduate social work students were similar.[18] Sharwell attributed such similarities to the selection process and also to professional socialization after these students were enrolled in their respective programs.[19]

Anticipated Value Profile of Beginning Social Work Students

It was anticipated that beginning social work students as a group would concur more with the four primary social work values represented in POS than would students in other related professions. It also was anticipated that graduate social work students, with their increased maturity and commitment to additional professional education, would concur more with the values than would undergraduate students.

The 583 students composing the sample reflected two primary categories used in the initial pilot testing of POS—(1) social work and (2) business—in addition to the following: at the undergraduate level, nursing, education, and related social sciences, specifically sociology and psychology; and at the graduate level, law, medicine, public policy, and education. Nursing, education, and business were selected as professions for which one can prepare during a typical four-year undergraduate program. Sociology and psychology were selected because many undergraduate students waver between them and social work before making a career choice. Graduates with sociology and psychology degrees frequently compete with BSWs in the job market. Law, medicine, education, and business were selected as major professions requiring at least two years of graduate education. Public policy was selected because, again, students often waver between it and social work before making a professional career choice.

Table 2.
Mean POS Value Scores of Beginning Undergraduate and Graduate Students

Type of Student	n	Value 1	Value 2	Value 3	Value 4
Undergraduate					
Social work	29	42.07	36.90	31.38	42.31
Business	48	38.81	34.23	24.90	39.69
Social science	19	40.11	37.11	29.26	41.11
Nursing	25	40.40	34.84	24.12	42.84
Education	22	40.45	34.36	25.86	41.68
Total	143				
Mean		40.17	35.28	26.80	41.27
Graduate					
Social work	194	42.75	37.62	30.66	43.26
Public policy	15	41.80	37.13	28.27	41.80
Medicine	65	39.62	34.02	28.82	41.35
Business	44	40.73	31.64	22.70	40.16
Law	95	41.31	33.35	28.54	41.67
Education	27	40.33	34.56	29.37	43.21
Total	440				
Mean		41.59	35.36	28.97	42.25

The size of the sample is delineated in Table 2. It should be noted that this represents a stratified sample that includes none of the subjects from the original pilot group. Subjects were procured from 21 different classes at three major northeastern universities during the fall 1985 semester.

Comparison of Beginning Social Work Students and Their Professional Counterparts

Students completed POS at the formal beginning of their professional education. For undergraduates, this was determined to be the first week of the junior year or that point at which they entered the majority of courses required for the major. Students selecting a major after this point would be required to spend additional time beyond the typical four-year span to complete the major requirements for graduation. For graduate students, this beginning point coincided with their first week of graduate school. A comparison of group means for each value of POS illustrates that, for the most part, both undergraduate and graduate social work students scored higher on the four value dimensions than their peers enrolled in other curricula (Table 2).

Further statistical analyses revealed that on the graduate level, the scores of the six professional groups were significantly different on all four value scales; scores of the five professional groups at the undergraduate level were

Table 3.
Significant Differences between Means of Beginning Social Work and Other Professional Students Based on Tukey's Honestly Significant Difference

Type of Student	Business Values: 1 2 3 4	Social Science/ Public Policy 1 2 3 4	Nursing/ Medicine 1 2 3 4	Education 1 2 3 4	Law 1 2 3 4
Undergraduate social work	*		*	*	
Graduate social work	* *		*		

* = p < .05.

also significantly different on all four value scales. Relevant F values and probability levels are summarized in Table A-13 in appendix A.

The value scale organization of POS appears to reflect the value hierarchy present in American society. Value 1—respect for basic rights—is a major focus of moral socialization emphasized in our educational system (see chapter 2). It also was the primary or most important scale identified by principal components factor analysis. Value 2—sense of social responsibility (or the second scale identified using principal components analysis)—flows from a strong respect for basic rights and is considered a necessary ingredient for moral decision making. Because all undergraduates participating had completed at least two years of their education and many of their general college requirements, it was not surprising that, as professional groups, they had less variability among their scores on values 1 and 2. Nor was it surprising that they exhibited greater variability on values 3 and 4, both of which are less highly emphasized in general college courses and more specifically as basic aspects of the social work curriculum (see Figure 3 for box-plots). These differences between values 1 and 2 and values 3 and 4 were not evident at the graduate level; rather, an examination of value scores of beginning graduate students revealed greater variability among all four value scores than occurs at the undergraduate level (Figure 4) (Table A-13, appendix A). This may be attributed to a variety of influences, such as greater differentiation of personal ideology or more pronounced personal preference because of experience and age.

A comparison of professional group means was performed using Tukey's Test of Honestly Significant Difference, a test designed to override the inherent bias in multiple comparisons of means (Table 3). It revealed that undergraduate social work students scored significantly higher on value 3 than did their business, nursing, and education counterparts. MSW students also scored significantly higher on value 1 than did the medical students

Figure 3.
Box-Plots for Value Scores of Beginning Undergraduate Students

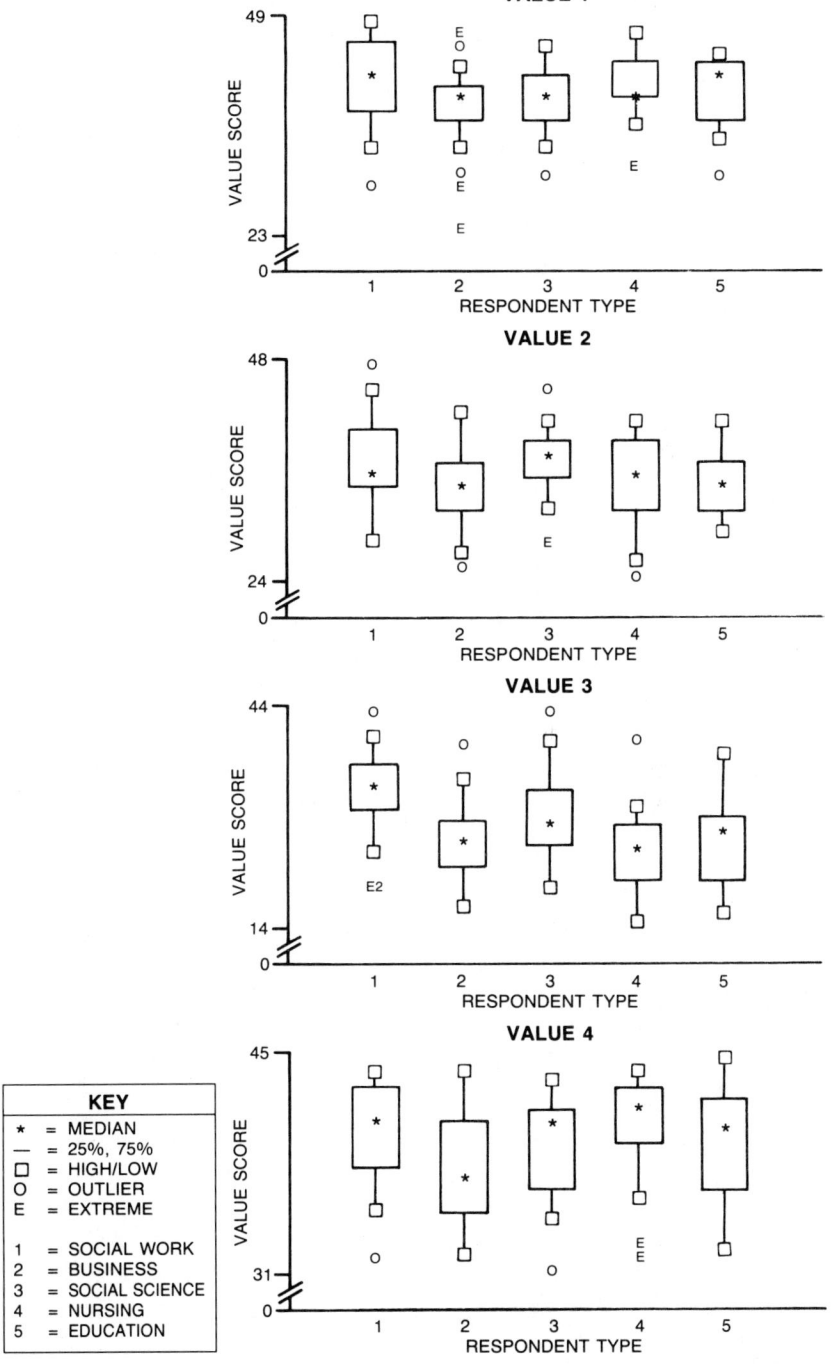

Figure 4.
Box-Plots for Value Scores of Beginning Graduate Students

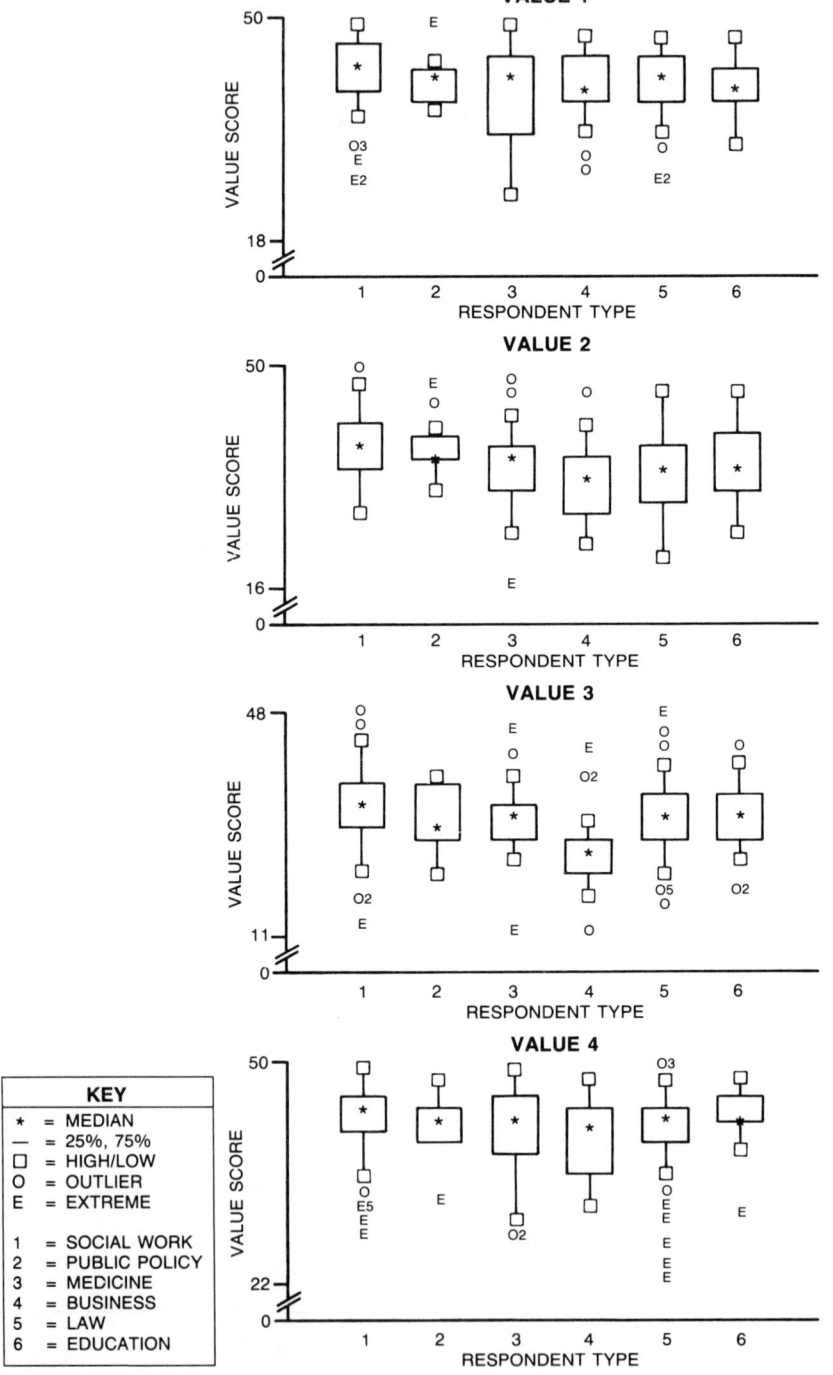

and higher on values 2 and 3 than did business students. As anticipated, undergraduate social work students were most like those students in related social sciences (sociology and psychology). Graduate students were most like students in public policy, education, and law, with no significant differences noted on any of the four values. BSW and MSW students did not differ significantly on any of the four values. It is important to note that the asterisks in Table 3 indicate significant differences ($p < .05$).

Explanation of Differences

What are some explanations for these differences? Are the differences noted between social work students and others related to gender? To religion? To age? To birthplace? To socioeconomic status?

Hayes and Varley, as well as Kidneigh and Lundberg, found that gender plays a significant role in student value/attitude differences.[20] On the whole, the values and attitudes of females tended to be more compatible with the underlying social work value base than were those of males. Cryns found that males in his study perceived people as significantly more altruistic, while females perceived people as more variable and individually distinct.[21]

One also would anticipate that religiosity or religious orientation would be related to student value/attitude differences. Because most religions have an underlying concern with helping others, religious involvement would be expected to increase concurrence with the underlying social work value base. It should be noted, however, that the degree of religiosity may have a bearing on attitudes, with the more strongly religious being concerned with the "afterlife" and the less religious being concerned with the "here-and-now," a stance more compatible with social work.

McLeod and Meyer found, in fact, that religious background was related to seven out of 10 of their designated social work values.[22] Interestingly, Protestants and Roman Catholics scored lower on all value dimensions; Jews and persons with no traditional religious commitment tended to score higher. This may be related to variation in concern with "afterlife."

It certainly would be anticipated that age is related to value and attitude differences. If one is a product of the sixties, one's value orientation should reflect that influence. People who are a product of the Great Depression most likely would have an orientation reflecting that influence. And if one is a product of the seventies, one should illustrate greater commitment to the "me" phenomenon, even though that influence may be minimized for those entering the profession of social work. In their sixties study, McLeod and Meyer found that age seemed to impact on two of their 10 value dimensions: persons over 30 scored slightly higher on group responsibility; persons under 30 scored slightly higher on diversity.[23]

Birthplace would be anticipated to have some bearing on value orientation. Society does give credence to a northern and a southern mentality, as well as to a rural–urban dichotomy. Hayes and Varley noted that regional culture appeared to have an impact on the value development of their sample of social work students.[24] Students from the North scored higher on aesthetic and social scales than did social work students from the South. The urban–rural dimension as related to students remains to be examined.

SES should have some bearing on the attitudes of social work students. In their study of social work students' attitudes toward the poor, Grimm and Orten found that the lower the student's SES, the less sympathetic were his or her attitudes toward the poor.[25] This finding is compatible with that suggested by Varley—that social work is based on middle-class values.[26] Thus, students from the middle SES should reflect values more compatible with those of the profession.

Student Differences

Neither the undergraduate nor graduate group of students was homogeneous (Table A-14, appendix A). Undergraduate students differed with respect to age, gender, political party affiliation, religion, and parents' educational levels; they did not differ significantly in terms of political philosophy or political activity level. Social workers tended to be older, with close to 50 percent being over 35. No business students were over 35; rather, the vast majority (95.7 percent) were under 25, a pattern similar to that in the other three undergraduate student groups (social science, education, and nursing). The business category had six times as many males as did social work and twice as many as social science. Education had twice as many males as social work and approximately one-third as many as business. More than 62 percent of the social work students were registered Democrats compared with 24 percent of the business students, 37 percent of the social science students, 41 percent of the nursing students, and 27 percent of the education students. Only slightly more than 3 percent of the social workers indicated no political party affiliation. This figure was seven to 10 times larger in the other professional groups. For all groups but those in education, Roman Catholicism was the principal religion; for those studying education, Protestantism was reported most frequently, followed by Roman Catholicism. At the undergraduate level, social science students tended to have the most highly educated parents, followed by business students; parents of social work students tended to cover the gamut, from having fewer than eight years of formal education to having completed graduate/professional school. Social work and nursing students had the highest percentage of parents with fewer than eight years of schooling.

Similar to undergraduate students, graduate social work students tended to be older than students in the other graduate groups. Social work, public policy, law, and education had a predominance of females; the reverse was true for medicine and business. Social work, public policy, and education reported the highest percentage of registered Democrats; graduate business students reported the highest percentage of Republicans. Social work students reported being more liberal politically than any other group, whereas business students described themselves as more conservative. Graduate students in public policy and business reported being most politically active. Medical and law students reported having the most highly educated parents; social work and public policy students reported the least educated parents.

Based on the foregoing, the following influences were examined by means of analyses of covariance: age, gender, religion, SES, and birthplace, as well as current region of residence. Additional analyses were conducted to examine the following: race, political party affiliation, political philosophy, and political activity level (Table A-15, appendix A). Undergraduate and graduate students were analyzed separately. When all of these variables were controlled for, graduate students in the various professional educational programs differed significantly on all four values. These findings, coupled with the results of Tukey's Honestly Significant Difference, present heightened evidence that social work students are, in fact, from the start, intrinsically different from those students who have entered into other professional programs.

It appeared that at the graduate level, family income was not a key factor. Underlying political philosophy, most likely an underdeveloped aspect of the lives of undergraduates, had the strongest impact on graduate students with respect to all four values. Gender and religion also played important roles in contributing to the variance of value scores. Current region of residence did contribute significantly to variance of value 1, as did the urban–rural dimension of the current residence, which contributed significantly to the variance of value 4 as well. Birthplace seemed to play a more significant role at the graduate level than at the undergraduate level. This may, in fact, have been more a function of age, with older (graduate) students having moved more often than the younger (undergraduate) students. This would explain why current residence played a more crucial role with undergraduate students.

At the undergraduate level, students in the various professions continued to exhibit significant differences on value 3 when controls were placed on the demographic variables. The demographic variable of primary importance to value 3 appeared to be age. As anticipated, both family income and religion played significant roles with respect to two values. Current region of residence played a significant role with respect to value 1. When the demographic variables were controlled at the undergraduate level, significant differences among the groups disappeared in three out of four values, thus reinforcing the importance of demographic variables. When the influence of demographic variables at the graduate level was controlled, significant differences among the groups remained or became accentuated, thus reinforcing the overall importance of professional type. The drastic difference between the two educational levels—undergraduate and graduate—may be the result of maturity and increased commitment to the profession. It can be assumed that pursuing an advanced degree does reflect additional commitment.

Social Work Students and Values

Social work students enter their profession with a greater concurrence with that underlying professional value base than do students entering other professional educational programs. This appears to be true at both the undergraduate and graduate levels, although different, specific demographic variables appear to account for the differences at the two educational levels. It should be safe to say that the influence of self-selection, coupled with the admissions process, has guaranteed that beginning social work students as a group are, in fact, more like members of that profession in their value orientation than are beginning students in a wide variety of related professions. Those professions at the graduate level include the following: law, medicine, education, business, and public policy. Those professions at the undergraduate level include the following: business, nursing, education, and related social sciences.

These results support the contention that beginning graduate students in social work express a greater commitment to the concept of basic rights, as well as a stronger commitment to social responsibility, individual freedom, and the concept of self-determination, than do their counterparts in other professional programs. Undergraduate social work students express a significantly stronger commitment to individual freedom than do students in other professional programs. Graduate students in general express a stronger commitment to all four basic social work values.

Both social work students themselves and social work educators appear to contribute to the selection of individuals who exhibit values that are more highly compatible with those of the profession. Of course, the key question is: What happens to those values as a result of the educational/professional socialization process? In what ways is their growth facilitated, stymied, or modified? What impact does work or life experience appear to exert? Although these students differ at the beginning, does that difference assure a similar differentiation and strengthening of commitment at the end of the educational process?

Notes and References

1. L. D. Barnard, "The Impact of the First Year of Professional Education in Social Work on Student Value Positions." Unpublished PhD dissertation, Bryn Mawr College, 1967.

2. Commission on Accreditation, "Appendix 1: Curriculum Policy for the Master's Degree and Baccalaureate Degree Programs in Social Work Education," *Handbook of Accreditation Standards and Procedures* (New York: Council on Social Work Education, 1984); and *Code of Ethics* (Washington, D.C.: National Association of Social Workers, Inc., 1980).

3. For an excellent overview of the role of individualism in our society, see D. B. James, *Poverty, Politics, and Change* (Englewood Cliffs, N.J.: Prentice-Hall, 1972); and R. N. Bellah et al., *Habits of the Heart* (New York: Harper & Row, 1985).

4. J. L. Vigilante, "Between Values and Science: Education for the Profession During a Moral Crisis or Is Proof Truth?" *Journal of Education for Social Work*, 10 (Fall 1974), pp. 107–115.

5. G. F. Koeske and M. A. Crouse, "Liberalism-Conservatism in Samples of Social Work Students and Professionals," *Social Service Review*, 55 (June 1981), pp. 193–205.

6. M. A. Taber and A. J. Vattano, "Clinical and Social Orientations in Social Work: An Empirical Study," *Social Service Review*, 44 (March 1970), pp. 34–43.

7. Koeske and Crouse, "Liberalism-Conservatism in Samples of Social Work Students and Professionals."

8. Bellah et al., *Habits of the Heart*, p. vii.

9. Ibid., chap. 10, "The National Society," pp. 250–271.

10. Ibid., p. 285.

11. James, *Poverty, Politics, and Change*.

12. J. C. Kidneigh and H. W. Lundberg, "Are Social Work Students Different?" *Social Work*, 3 (July 1958), pp. 57–61.

13. Koeske and Crouse, "Liberalism-Conservatism in Samples of Social Work Students and Professionals."

14. J. M. Gustafson, "Professions as 'Callings,'" *Social Service Review*, 56 (December 1982), pp. 501–515.

15. D. D. Hayes and B. K. Varley, "Impact of Social Work Education on Students' Values," *Social Work*, 10 (July 1965), pp. 40–46.

16. Kidneigh and Lundberg, "Are Social Work Students Different?"

17. G. R. Sharwell, "Can Values Be Taught? A Study of Two Variables Related to Orientation of Social Work Graduate Students Toward Public Dependency," *Journal of Education for Social Work*, 10 (Spring 1974), pp. 99–105.

18. A. G. Cryns, "Social Work Education and Student Ideology: A Multivariate Study of Professional Socialization," *Journal of Education for Social Work*, 13 (Winter 1977), pp. 44–51.

19. Sharwell, "Can Values Be Taught?"

20. Hayes and Varley, "Impact of Social Work Education on Students' Values"; and Kidneigh and Lundberg, "Are Social Work Students Different?"

21. Cryns, "Social Work Education and Student Ideology."
22. D. L. McLeod and H. J. Meyer, "Chapter 30: A Study of the Values of Social Workers," in E. J. Thomas, ed., *Behavioral Science for Social Workers* (New York: Free Press, 1967), pp. 401–416.
23. Ibid.
24. Hayes and Varley, "Impact of Social Work Education on Students' Values."
25. J. W. Grimm and J. D. Orten, "Student Attitudes Toward the Poor," *Social Work,* 18 (January 1973), pp. 94–100.
26. B. K. Varley, "Socialization in Social Work Education," *Social Work,* 8 (July 1963), pp. 102–109.

F · O · U · R

Education:
Its Contribution to Professional Socialization

♦

The primary means to becoming a member of a profession is by identifying with one's mentors or colleagues.[1] As Noble and King noted, "Professional values and ethics form an important unifying bond in our widely diversified...profession and impart identity and meaning to it.... Social work is concerned with the values that give direction to our efforts, and social work educators view the transmission of professional values and ethics as singularly important."[2] Social work educators must have an understanding of the underlying values and design curricula to foster this "we" feeling or sense of identification. This educational piece consists of several major parts: curriculum content, exposure to faculty and field instructors, and the influence of peers. According to standards for program accreditation (for both BSW and MSW programs) espoused by CSWE,[3] the following six content areas must be addressed by successful (accreditable) programs: (1) social work research, (2) human behavior in the social environment, (3) social welfare policy, (4) social work practice, (5) respect for cultural diversity, and (6) *social work values* [italics added]. The respect for cultural diversity and social work values content areas should permeate or be present throughout the first four content areas. Not only should they be evident in course syllabi, but their presence also should be highlighted in field practicum objectives as well as in overall program goals and objectives. As Hokenstad wrote, "The values and principles that guide professional social workers...should be manifest throughout every social work curriculum."[4]

An examination of a sample of basic social work texts reveals that values are treated as part of a "golden" triumvirate necessary for successful social work practice: skills, knowledge, and values, with values being the overriding guardians of ethical practice. Shulman defines practice theory as being based on knowledge about human behavior and social organization, underlying assumptions (or values—author's interpretation) about goals and outcomes, and specified workers' actions.[5] Pincus and Minahan define *social work practice* as action grounded on both values and knowledge.[6] In defining *casework,* a psychosocial therapy, Hollis and Woods clearly state that it must rest on a particular value base.[7] Knowledge about human behavior, systems theory, and personality, combined with that value base, serve as a guide to therapeutic intervention. Garvin and Seabury define social work practice along similar dimensions. They view it as being "guided by three types of information. ...human behavior and its social setting; ...ethics and values of the profession; ...the 'action repertoire.' "[8]

To succeed in his [her] chosen profession, the neophyte must make an...adjustment to the professional culture... wherein he [she] internalizes the social values, the behavioral norms, and the symbols of the occupational group...no different from the acculturation of an immigrant to a relatively strange culture.
   —E. Greenwood, "Attributes of a Profession," *Social Work,* 2 (July 1957), pp. 44–55.

To become socialized into the profession or to increase one's identification with one's mentors or senior colleagues, one should exhibit evidence not only of increased theoretical knowledge and professional practice skills but also of increased assimilation of the underlying social work value base espoused by members of the profession. As noted in chapter 3, neophytes come to the social work profession exhibiting a greater commitment to its value base than do individuals selecting other professions. It is impossible to determine which plays the greater role in promoting this factor: self-selection by applicants, along with the influence of "anticipatory socialization," or the application screening processes employed by various social work educational programs. ("Anticipatory socialization" is the term coined by Hayes and Varley to describe a would-be professional's tendency to identify with his or her chosen group.[9]) One thing is evident: those entering social work programs exhibit greater concurrence with the following social work values—respect for basic rights, sense of social responsibility, commitment to individual freedom, and support of self-determination—as measured by POS. When controls are exerted on the influence of age; SES;

religion; political party affiliation; political activity level; gender; race; region of birth as well as current residence (e.g., rural versus urban, north versus south); and family income, significant differences continue to exist.

If professional educational programs serve their objectives, those completing them should exhibit greater professional socialization than those just beginning them. Recent social work graduates should exhibit greater concurrence with professional social work values than students beginning in such curricula, as well as graduates of other related professional curricula.

Social Work Education and Value Change and Assimilation

A number of researchers have examined the impact of social work education on value change as well as on degree of value assimilation. In examining value orientation, McLeod and Meyer found that on all 10 values they measured, trained social workers and those in training scored higher than untrained social workers.[10] They attempted to determine whether other characteristics were more important than social work education. When the amount of nonprofessional or general education was held constant, significant differences continued to exist among the three groups. Age appeared to have no bearing; religion, on the other hand, appeared to be related to seven out of 10 values. Ethnic background also appeared to be related to value differences; however, the possible interrelationship between religion and ethnicity must be considered. McLeod and Meyer extended their study by comparing social workers with teachers. On all educational levels, social workers scored higher on all 10 value dimensions than did the teachers. Based on these findings, McLeod and Meyer suggested the need to compare social workers with members of other professions.

In comparing beginning MSW students with recent graduates, Varley found no significant differences on the following four individual value dimensions: (1) equal rights, (2) service, (3) psychodynamic-mindedness, and (4) universalism.[11] When the four values were combined for a total value score, however, significant differences were noted. Interestingly, Varley found that age was a critical factor in the socialization process; younger students showed the greatest positive change in value scores and older students, the smallest change.

Using Hollinghead's Two Factor Index as a basis for determining SES,[12] Varley found SES to be an important determinant, with students from upper-SES groups showing the least change and those from lower-SES groups, the most. Two-thirds of the students, who were from middle-SES groups, exhibited minimal value change; this outcome was to be expected if, in fact, social work is based on middle-class values.

Varley also found work experience to be related to value change. Students who had no professional social work experience exhibited the greatest change, and those who held social work positions or who had previous exposure to social workers showed the least change. This not only speaks to the importance of practical experience in determining and molding values, it also speaks to the need for competency-based education, especially for experienced workers returning to school for a graduate degree. Such students may not need the same type or amount of professional socialization as a neophyte embarking on a professional career.

In a later study designed to examine the impact of education on professional socialization, Varley found that students entering graduate programs were more committed to social work values than were experienced social workers.[13] By the end of their educational experience, they exhibited negative changes or reduced commitment to three out of four values. None of the independent variables alone was able to differentiate between graduates whose value scores changed in a positive direction and those whose scores changed in a negative direction. Two characteristics taken together (age and prior social work experience) produced trends. Older students without prior experience had the least negative change; younger students without experience had the greatest negative change. Although this may appear alarming, it does support the concept of professional socialization; that is, younger, inexperienced students may have entered the program more strongly committed to service and universalism than did experienced workers. In fact, their orientation may have been unrealistic and overly zealous. By graduation, their views may have been modified (undergone negative change) to be more compatible with the views espoused by the experienced workers. Older, inexperienced students may have started out with views that were more compatible with those of experienced professionals. Thus, the degree of and/or need for professional socialization may have been reduced. The data support the influence or role of education in value assimilation or socialization, with the outcome being greater approximation of the value orientation of more experienced professionals, the "we" to whom students aspire.

One concern Varley noted was the possible lack of consistent direction in defining curriculum guidelines to facilitate value development. Another concern was that faculty and field instructors were not presenting a united front with respect to values. Although that concern continues, the increased focus on values offered by the CSWE Accreditation Standards and the CSWE Curriculum Policy Statements,[14] coupled with increased attention to values by NASW,[15] may foster a more uniform emphasis. Considering the timetable, it was studies such as those by Varley that were the impetus for increased emphasis on values by CSWE and NASW. Studies such as the current one will evaluate the effectiveness of such program modifications in fostering positive value assimilation and professional socialization.

In comparing beginning and graduating social work students, Hayes and Varley found a small difference between them, with education facilitating a commitment to equal rights and possibly a rejection of the values labeled service, universalism, and psychodynamic-mindedness.[16] Sharwell, on the other hand, compared student and graduate attitudes toward public dependency and found that beginning students and graduates did differ significantly.[17] He attributed this to professional socialization resulting from professional education as well as the selection process. It is important to note, however, that the educational program he studied was designed specifically around issues related to public dependency. Thus one finds that his study suggests that a focused curriculum can produce change or socialization in the desired direction.

In examining the attitudes of MSW students toward the poor, Grimm and Orten found socioeconomic background and prior work experience to be important determinants.[18] They also suggested that students' attitudes may not be neutralized (modified) by the relatively short period of professional socialization offered by educational programs. They found that the lower the SES of students, the less sympathetic their attitudes were toward the poor. They also found that positive attitudes toward the poor were associated with an undergraduate degree in sociology or social work, and from a public university or school in some place *other* than the South.

Several important trends were noted. First, in most instances, education does have an impact on values, whether in a positive or negative direction; education plays a significant role in professional socialization. Second, social work graduates exhibit a stronger commitment to social work values than do students or graduates in other professions. They also exhibit greater concurrence with social work values than do beginning social work students. In addition, professional social work experience facilitates value change; age, religion, and SES appear to be related to differences in value orientation. However, one distinct factor should be noted: all studies reported here were conducted before publication of the 1983/84 CSWE Curriculum Policy Statements and the 1984 CSWE Accreditation Standards. All studies predate the 1980 version of the NASW *Code of Ethics.* All the studies used measurement instruments based on limited tests of reliability and validity. Rather than focusing on the broad spectrum of values, some data collection instruments focused on specific issues, such as attitudes toward the poor or toward public dependency.

Focus

The present focus measures the impact of education on value orientation by using larger samples than did previous studies. It also uses an instrument that was based on higher levels of reliability and validity and designed specifically to measure the four social work values reflected in the current NASW Public Social Policy Statements. The study also was designed to reexamine the influence of the following demographic variables on value orientation as related to recent graduates: gender, age, race, SES based on both father's educational level and current family income, geographic region of origin, current residence, political activity level, political philosophy, and religion.

Based on previous findings, coupled with the current emphasis on values in social work education, it was anticipated that graduates who recently completed requirements for a degree in social work would concur more with the four professional values measured by POS than would either beginning social work students or graduates in other professions. Because of the role played by social work faculty and field instructors in the process of professional socialization, it also was anticipated that the values of recent social work graduates would be more similar to those of faculty and field instructors than would those of beginning social work students or of graduates of other professional programs.

For purposes of comparison, the following professions were selected: at the undergraduate level, education, business, and nursing; at the graduate level, education, law, and business; and medicine. During the month after they completed their degrees, graduates of the various programs were asked to complete POS. The mailed response rates ranged from almost 28 percent for graduates in social work and business (at both undergraduate and graduate levels) to 14 percent for those in law and almost 10 percent for those in medicine. Rates for education were about 24 percent and 21 percent for nursing.

Recent Graduates

Subjects included a total of 363 from three major universities in the Northeast; half recently had received undergraduate degrees and half, graduate degrees. Details of the respondent group are summarized in Table 4. The respondent group represents a random stratified sample that includes none of the respondents from the pilot testing. Table 4 also presents an overview of the POS value score means for the 1986 graduates representing each professional group. For the most part, social work graduates scored higher on all four values than did graduates in other professional groups. The only exception was in nursing, with its mean score for value 4.

Further statistical analyses revealed that the variance of scores of graduates from the various professional groups was significantly different on all four values (Table A-16, appendix A, presents relevant F scores and probability levels). Box-plots clearly illustrate a comparison of the value score variances both for graduates of the undergraduate professional programs (Figure 5) and for graduates of the various graduate curricula (Figure 6).

A comparison of professional group means was conducted using Tukey's Test of Honestly Significant Difference, which is designed to override the inherent bias in multiple comparisons of means. Results revealed that

Education: Its Contribution to Professional Socialization

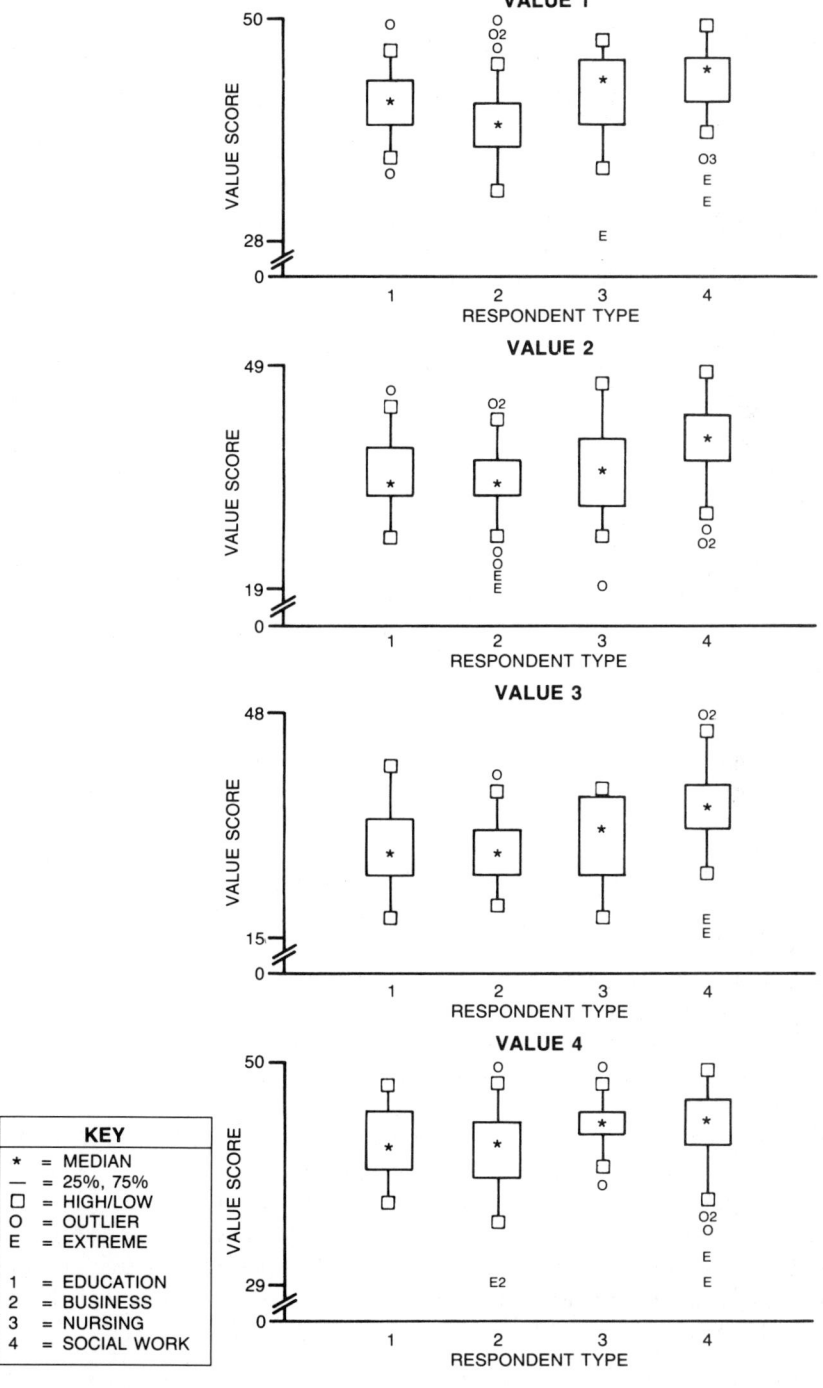

Figure 5.
Box-Plots for Value Scores of Graduates of Undergraduate Professional Programs

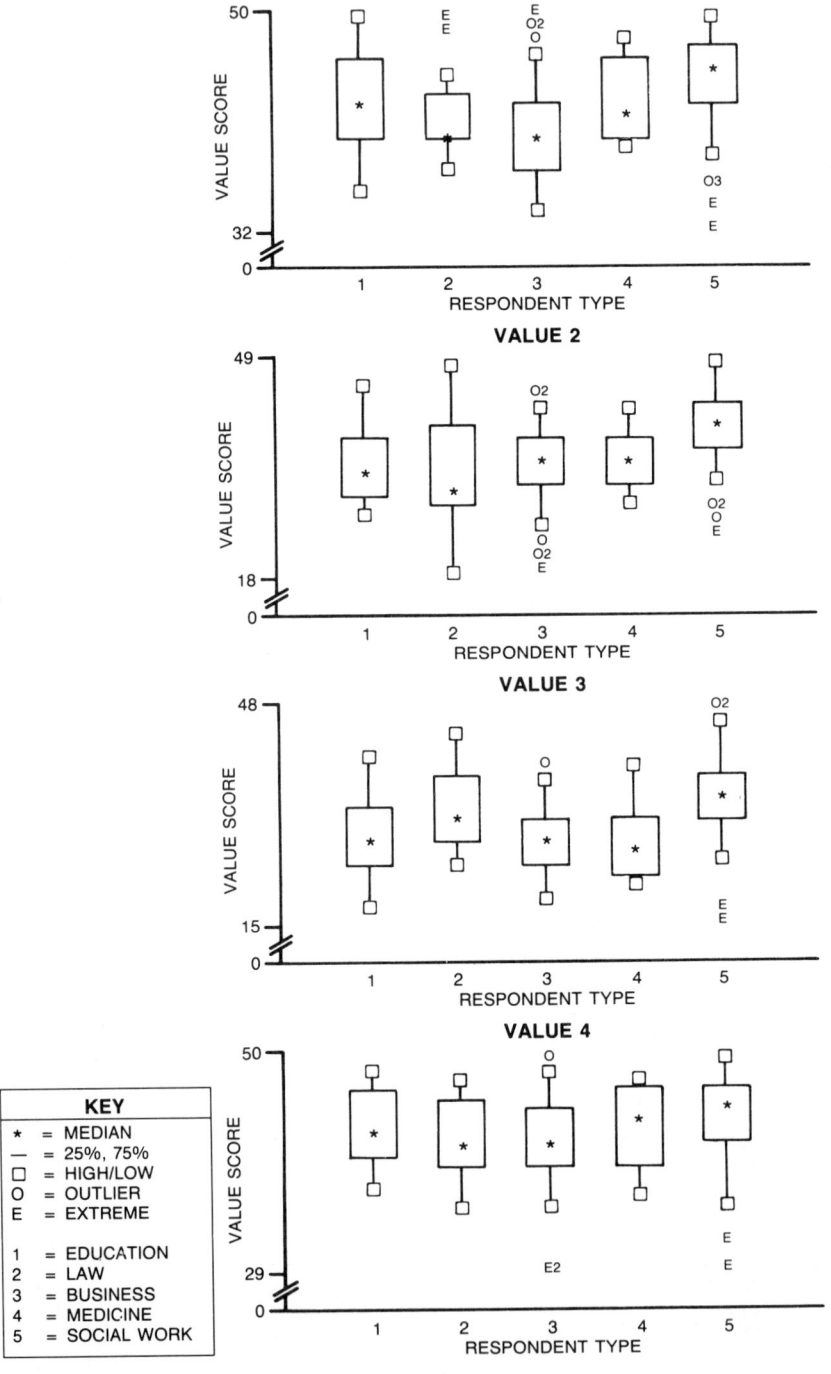

Figure 6.
Box-Plots for Value Scores of Graduates of Graduate Professional Programs

Table 4.
POS Value Score Means for 1986 Graduates Representing Each Professional Group

Type of Graduate	n	Value 1	Value 2	Value 3	Value 4
Undergraduate					
Social work	94	44.18	39.35	33.03	43.88
Education	25	42.72	34.84	26.68	42.92
Business	41	40.27	33.37	26.24	41.12
Nursing	21	43.10	34.57	27.43	44.62
Total	181				
Mean		42.97	36.82	29.96	43.21
Graduate					
Social work	91	44.13	39.25	33.20	43.81
Education	23	42.74	34.57	26.91	43.22
Business	43	40.21	33.21	26.28	41.05
Medicine	12	41.58	34.42	26.08	43.17
Law	13	41.54	32.62	30.31	41.31
Total	182				
Mean		42.68	36.44	30.09	42.86

business graduates (at the undergraduate level) differed significantly from social work graduates on all four values and that education and nursing graduates differed significantly from social work graduates on values 2 and 3 (Table 5). At the graduate level, business graduates differed significantly from social work graduates on values 1, 2, and 3. Education graduates and physicians differed significantly from MSWs on values 2 and 3; and law graduates differed significantly on value 2.

It is important to compare these findings with those reported in chapter 3 on beginning students (Table 3). More significant differences were noted

Table 5.
Significant Differences between Means of Social Work and Other Professions (1986 Graduates) Based on Tukey's Honestly Significant Difference

Type of Graduate Values:	Education 1 2 3 4	Business 1 2 3 4	Nursing/ Medicine 1 2 3 4	Law 1 2 3 4
Undergraduate social work	* *	* * * *	* *	
Graduate social work	* *	* * *	* *	*

* = $p < .05$.

in comparing graduates of social work programs and their peers in related professions than in comparing beginning students in the various professional groups.

Differences among the Graduates

Table A-17 in appendix A presents a summary of chi-square analyses identifying demographic differences among recent graduates. The results indicate that neither graduates of undergraduate professional degree programs nor graduates of graduate programs could be considered homogeneous groups.

Graduates at the undergraduate level differed significantly in gender. Educators and businesspeople, proportionally, had more than twice as many males as did nursing and social work. In political party affiliation, business had three times as many registered Republicans as did social work, almost twice as many as education, and eight times as many as nursing. Social work had by far more registered Democrats than did any other group. Education and nursing had more than twice as many independents as either business or social work. In political philosophy, almost 38 percent of the social workers described themselves as liberal and 57 percent as moderate; 24 percent of the business graduates referred to themselves as liberal and 56 percent as moderate. Proportionally, three times as many business graduates as social workers described themselves as conservative.

More graduates in education than in any other group had a father with a graduate degree (36 percent); business graduates reported slightly more than 7 percent in this category, nursing twice that amount, and social work, 17 percent. Only 8 percent of education graduates reported having a father who did not have a high school diploma; on the other hand, 36 percent of the social work graduates, 34 percent of those in nursing, and 39 percent of the business graduates reported similarly. No significant differences were noted on their mother's educational level. Religion, which was significant among beginning undergraduate students, was no longer significant among recent graduates. Political philosophy, which was not significant among beginning students, emerged as significant among recent graduates of undergraduate professional programs.

At the graduate level, lawyers and physicians tended to be younger, in general, although they both reported the smallest percentage under age 25. Graduates in education, business, and social work all reported large percentages over age 45 (22 percent, 30 percent, and 20 percent, respectively). Business and medicine had by far the highest percentages of males (37.2 percent and 41.7 percent, respectively) in comparison with the other three professions; social work had the lowest percentage of males (14.3 percent).

Significant differences among recent graduates at the graduate level were noted in their political party affiliation. Graduates in social work, medicine, and law had the highest percentage of registered Democrats, with 63.7 percent, 58.3 percent, and 46.2 percent, respectively. Business reported the largest percentage of registered Republicans (37.2 percent), followed by medicine (25 percent) and education (21.7 percent). Education reported an unusually high percentage of independents (34.8 percent). Almost 36 percent of recent MSW degree recipients reported being liberal in comparison with graduates in education (13 percent); law (23 percent); business (23 percent); and medicine (16 percent). At the opposite extreme, social work had the smallest percentage describing themselves as conservative (6.7 percent); followed by education (13 percent); law (15.4 percent); business (21 percent); and medicine (none).

Recent graduates of the various graduate degree programs also differed significantly in current family income. Beginning lawyers and those people with a master of business administration (MBA) degree reported the highest family incomes; social workers, educators, and physicians reported the lowest family incomes. The physicians' low incomes no doubt result from the fact that they all were in internships, which carry relatively low salaries. Graduates also differed significantly in their parents' educational levels. Having a father with a graduate degree was reported by educators (30.4 percent); lawyers (30.8 percent); and physicians (41.7 percent). Social workers (17.6 percent) and business graduates (7.0 percent) reported far lower paternal educational levels. Proportionally, more MSWs (36.3 percent) and MBAs (39.6 percent) reported having a father who did not have a high school diploma. No significant differences were noted in their mother's educational level.

Analysis of Demographic Influences

When the influence of various demographic variables (age, gender, race, political philosophy, religion, birthplace, current region of residence, rural versus urban dimensions, and SES as measured by father's occupation and current family income) was controlled, the variance of the value scores of the professional groupings continued to differ significantly on all four value scales (Table A-18 in appendix A). These results support the fact that both BSW and MSW social work graduates have a significantly different value orientation than that of graduates of other professional programs, and not a different orientation owing to specific demographic differences.

The most important variable contributing to group differences at both the graduate and undergraduate levels was political philosophy, followed by family income and gender at the undergraduate level, and race and gender at the graduate level. Other significant covariates at the undergraduate level were current residence and race; and at the graduate level, family income and religion. These variables support those uncovered by previous research efforts, such as findings noted earlier in this chapter.

Table 6.
Comparison of Group Value Means for Beginning Social Work Students, Recent Graduates, Faculty, Field Instructors, and Agency Personnel

	n	Value 1	Value 2	Value 3	Value 4
Undergraduate level					
Beginning	29	41.83	36.90	32.28	42.31
Graduates	94	44.28	39.35	34.23	43.88
Graduate level					
Beginning	194	42.62	37.62	32.02	43.26
Graduates	91	44.29	39.25	43.35	43.81
Social work faculty	21	44.11	39.89	35.58	44.17
Field instructors	15	43.93	39.82	36.08	43.65
Agency personnel	118	43.18	38.09	34.40	42.87

Comparison of Recent Graduates and Beginning Professionals

A primary concern in examining the impact of education on value orientation is a comparison of recent graduates with beginners and/or seasoned practitioners—in this case, faculty, field instructors, and agency personnel. If educational curricula serve the underlying purpose of professional socialization, recent graduates should be more similar in value orientation to experienced workers, including faculty and field instructors, than beginning students should be.

In comparisons of group value score means of beginning students, recent graduates, faculty, field instructors, and agency personnel, graduates, on the whole, were more like seasoned practitioners than were beginning students (Table 6). In comparing group means, it was found that beginning social work students differed significantly from faculty on values 1, 2, and 3 (Table 7). The fact that these differences disappeared by the time of graduation implied that a certain amount of socialization had taken place. Note that the faculty and field instructors included are those who provided the primary professional socialization for the recent social work graduates being examined.

Graduates from undergraduate social work programs did differ significantly from beginning students in education, nursing, and business; graduates from graduate social work programs differed from beginning students in education, medicine, law, and business on many value scores. An examination of Table 3 illustrates that minimal differences were evident between beginning social work students and those entering the other professional training programs. The greater differences at the time of graduation offer additional evidence of the socialization that had taken place between

Table 7.
Comparison of Value Scores of Beginning Students and Graduates with Each Other and with Faculty, Field Instructors, and Social Service Agency Personnel[a]

Type of Student Values:	1986 Graduates				Faculty				Field				Agency			
	1	2	3	4	1	2	3	4	1	2	3	4	1	2	3	4
Undergraduate																
Beginning students																
Education	*	*	*		*	*			*	*			*			
Nursing	*	*	*		*	*			*	*			*			
Business	*	*	*	*	*	*	*	*	*	*	*	*	*	*		
Social work					*	*	*									
1986 graduates in social work																
Graduates																
Beginning students																
Education	*				*	*			*	*						
Medicine	*	*			*	*			*	*						
Law	*				*				*	*			*	*		
Business	*	*			*	*			*	*	*		*	*		
Social work					*	*	*									
1986 graduates in social work																

* = $p < .05$.
[a]Differences between 1986 social work graduates and graduates of other professional programs are reported in Table 5.

entrance to and completion of the two professional social work programs (BSW and MSW). The asterisks in Table 7 indicate significant differences between the value means of the groups being compared ($p < .05$).

Some additional differences undoubtedly were disguised or influenced by the presence of assorted demographic variables examined by analyses of covariance (Table A-18, appendix A). Additional examination of the impact of such variables is presented in chapter 6.

Effects of Education on Value Orientation

Based on these findings, it was concluded that professional social work education does have an important impact on the professional socialization of students, especially in the area of value orientation. Both graduate and undergraduate students entered the program with values significantly different from those of the social work faculty (Table 7). By graduation, these value differences had disappeared. Differences between social work and the other professional groups that had been identified at the beginning of their educational careers (Table 3) became more pronounced by graduation (Table 5); additional differences also were identified. By graduation, social work graduates were remarkably more unlike beginning students in other professional groups (Table 7), as well as being significantly different from their peers graduating from the other professions as measured by comparisons of group means (Table 5). In other professional programs, such professional socialization was not evident. Although students in those programs most likely changed along many dimensions throughout their academic careers, they did not change in the same way as the social work students did in their relative concurrence with the social work values measured by POS.

This lack of value change by the students in the other professional programs is somewhat surprising; the majority of the other professional educational curricula are guided by specific program accreditation criteria, some of which emphasize values akin to those espoused by social work. For example, the curriculum accreditation guidelines for nursing developed by the National League for Nursing stress that nursing students must be exposed to the legal, historical, political, social, economic, and ethical aspects of nursing.[19] Included in this is a familiarity with the "Patients' Bill of Rights," which includes the concept of "informed consent," the "right to die," and patients' rights in research, including the concept of confidentiality. Throughout the curriculum, especially in clinical courses, nurses are exposed to the content of the American Nurses Association (ANA) *Code for Nurses.*[20] Critical aspects of that code include provision of service "based on respect for human dignity and unrestricted by social or economic status, personal attributes, or the nature of the health problems."[21] The International Council of Nurses also includes in its code "respect for life, dignity, and the rights of man."[22]

Standards for accreditation of medical education curricula, governed by the Liaison Committee on Medical Education, demand that an accredited medical school curriculum "be designed to instill in its graduates the knowledge and skills fundamental to the practice of medicine. In addition, the curriculum also must instill lifelong habits of learning, dedication to service and the values and attitudes consistent with a compassionate profession."[23] Additionally, medical education accreditation guidelines indicate that accredited programs "must teach ethical, behavioral, and socioeconomic subjects pertinent to medicine. There should be presentations of material on medical ethics and human values."[24]

Law schools, which are accredited by both the American Association of Law Schools and the American Bar Association (ABA), must "require of all candidates for the first professional degree, instruction in the duties and responsibilities of the legal profession. Such required instruction need not be limited to any pedagogical method as long as the history, goals, structure and responsibilities of the legal profession and its members, including the American Bar Association Model Code of Professional Responsibility, are all covered."[25] All accredited law schools now require a course in "professional responsibility"; however, student receptivity to and appreciation of such courses have been mixed.[26]

While business curricula accreditation criteria mention social responsibility, such criteria appear to place less emphasis on it. The accreditation guidelines of the American Assembly of Collegiate Schools of Business state that the "purpose of the curriculum shall be to provide for a broad education preparing the student for imaginative and responsible citizenship and leadership roles in business and society—domestic and worldwide."[27]

The general standards for eligibility to teach indicate that (candidates) "must be of good moral character." Although each of the various programs places some emphasis on values, not one places as much emphasis on the values measured by POS as does social work. In the Standards for Accreditation developed by the National Council for Accreditation of Teacher Education, minimal attention is directed to concern with values and other related topics, such as cultural diversity. Standard I-C-3 states that "courses and experiences support the development of independent thinking, effective communication, the making of relevant judgments, professional collaboration, effective participation in the educational systems, and the discrimination of values in the educational arena."[28] In addition, Standard III.A (Admission) states, "The unit's admission procedures encourage the recruitment of a culturally diverse student population."[29]

Although the samples used here are small and are not representative of a variety of programs, the results suggest that educational programs do play a significant part in professional socialization. The use of national samples would increase the generalizability of the results. Although exposed to the same educational program, faculty, and field instructors, the beginning students and recent graduates examined here represented two mutually exclusive samples. The use of longitudinal samples also would enhance the quality of the research.

Despite the preceding limitations, the results support the impact of education on professional socialization, especially as it relates to value orientation. It appears that during their professional education, social work students develop a value orientation that is more compatible with that espoused by the faculty orchestrating and providing that educational experience. A concern that remains to be examined, however, is the specific impact each of the various educational dimensions contributes to the socialization process. Of course, the term "socialization" in itself may be somewhat misleading. It implies that students are passive learners, wholly receptive to new values. Obviously, educators are encouraged to provide appropriate value-enhancing curriculum components. Certainly the goals of social work educational programs are such that proposed value assimilation is rewarded and encouraged; the opposite is clearly dissuaded and negatively reinforced. Most important, and perhaps hardest to examine, is the strong predisposition of social work students to become more like the professional group to which they aspire.

Earlier research noted the need for a decrease in value scores for recent graduates to become more like their professors and other seasoned professionals. In this case, it was necessary for value scores to increase to approximate the scores of those experienced individuals more closely. The phenomenon may be unique to the social workers involved here, or it may reflect the very nature of POS.

Notes and References

1. W. W. Boehm, *Objectives of the Social Work Curriculum of the Future* (New York: Council on Social Work Education, 1959), p. 20.

2. D. N. Noble and J. E. King, "Values: Passing on the Torch Without Burning the Runner," *Social Casework*, 62 (December 1981), pp. 579–584.

3. Commission on Accreditation, *Handbook of Accreditation Standards and Procedures* (New York: Council on Social Work Education, 1984).

4. M. C. Hokenstad, "Preparation for Practice: The Ethical Dimension," *Social Work Education Reporter*, 35 (1987), p. 1.

5. L. Shulman, *The Skills of Helping Individuals and Groups* (2d ed.; Itasca, Ill.: F. E. Peacock Publishers, 1984), p. 3.

6. A. Pincus and A. Minahan, *Social Work Practice: Model and Method* (Itasca, Ill.: F. E. Peacock Publishers, 1973), p. 38.

7. F. Hollis and M. E. Woods, *Casework: A Psychosocial Therapy* (3d ed.; New York: Random House, 1981), and chap. 2, "The Psychosocial Frame of Reference," pp. 25–55.

8. C. D. Garvin and B. A. Seabury, *Interpersonal Practice in Social Work: Processes and Procedures* (Englewood Cliffs, N.J.: Prentice-Hall, 1984), p. 2.

9. D. D. Hayes and B. K. Varley, "Impact of Social Work Education on Students' Values," *Social Work*, 10 (July 1965), pp. 40–46.

10. D. L. McLeod and H. J. Meyer, "Chapter 30: A Study of the Values of Social Workers," in E. J. Thomas, ed., *Behavioral Science for Social Workers* (New York: Free Press, 1967), pp. 401–416.

11. B. K. Varley, "Socialization in Social Work Education," *Social Work*, 8 (July 1963), pp. 102–109.

12. A. B. Hollingshead and F. C. Redlich, *Social Class and Mental Illness* (New York: John Wiley & Sons, 1958).

13. B. K. Varley, "Social Work Values: Changes in Value Commitments of Students from Admission to MSW Graduation," *Journal of Education for Social Work*, 14 (Fall 1968), pp. 67–76.

14. Commission on Accreditation, *Handbook of Accreditation Standards and Procedures*.

15. Several indications of the increased concern about values and ethics on the part of NASW is evidenced by the following. In 1964, NASW established the National Committee on Inquiry, an official body designed to handle complaints about the ethical practices of specific members. In 1970, the Committee on Inquiry presented the first version of procedures for adjudication, which subsequently were revised in 1978 and currently are under revision. The revised version is slated for completion in 1988. The NASW *Code of Ethics,* most recently revised in 1980, has been revised regularly to reflect the increased emphasis on ethical behavior stemming from the underlying professional value base.

16. Hayes and Varley, "Impact of Social Work Education on Students' Values."

17. G. R. Sharwell, "Can Values Be Taught? A Study of Two Variables Related to Orientation of Social Work Graduate Students Toward Public Dependency," *Journal of Education for Social Work,* 10 (Spring 1974), pp. 99–105.

18. J. W. Grimm and J. D. Orten, "Student Attitudes Toward the Poor," *Social Work,* 18 (January 1973), pp. 94–100.

19. *See Criteria for the Evaluation of Baccalaureate and Higher Degree Programs in Nursing* (5th ed.; New York: National League for Nursing, 1983).

20. *For a discussion of the National League for Nursing and the American Nurses' Association, see* L. Y. Kelly, *Dimensions of Professional Nursing* (4th ed.; New York: Macmillan Publishing Co., 1981), chaps. 25–26.

21. *See* American Nurses Association, *Code for Nurses* (1976), as cited in Kelly, *Dimensions of Professional Nursing,* p. 174.

22. Ibid., p. 175.

23. Liaison Committee on Medical Education, *Functions and Structure of a Medical School: Standards for Accreditation of Medical Education Programs Leading to the M.D. Degree* (Chicago: Association of American Medical Colleges and the American Medical Association, 1985), p. 1.

24. Ibid., p. 13.

25. *Standards for Approval of Law Schools and Interpretations* (Indianapolis: American Bar Association, 1986), standard 302.a.iv.

26. *See* E. G. Gee and D. W. Jackson, "Current Studies of Legal Education: Findings and Recommendations," *Journal of Legal Education,* 32 (December 1982), pp. 471–505.

27. *Accreditation Council Policies, Procedures, and Standards* (St. Louis, Mo.: American Assembly of Collegiate Schools of Business, 1986–87), p. 28.

28. *Standards, Procedures, Policies for the Accreditation of Professional Education Units* (Washington, D.C.: National Council for Accreditation of Teacher Education, 1968), p. 29.

29. Ibid., p. 34.

F · I · V · E

Time in the Trenches:
Orientation of Seasoned Professionals

◆

To know a person, one must understand that individual's profession and its basic underlying philosophy. To understand how someone relates to that profession, one must have not only a grasp of professional expectations but also a feel for the impact or influence of that individual's basic underlying dynamics and beliefs. The two—professional self and personal self—are never mutually exclusive; rather, they intertwine to form one's total entity. One's basic personality may influence the selection of a profession; one's profession definitely influences the course and direction of one's personal life, to say nothing of influencing and expanding one's basic values.

To understand how various professionals relate to one another, how business is conducted in everyday life, one must understand the similarities and differences among the various professions. These are the internal rules and expectations, the rules for interacting with members of one's own profession and of other professions; the rules for interacting with clients; and, finally, society's expectations of various professions, the rules that take precedence over one's personal values.[1]

To become a bona fide member of a profession takes time, energy, and ability. Time is needed to acquire necessary knowledge; to understand the rules of the game, the values, the expectations; to assimilate the traits associated with the profession; and to become accepted as a member of the profession by other members, by consumers of professional services, and by society in general. Energy and grim determination also are critical, as are intellectual ability and necessary financial resources. As noted in the various educational program accreditation criteria, different programs have different educational requirements (chapter 4) just as the different professions have varying requirements for membership. Although similarities exist among the professions, differences can be identified readily.

To understand men [women] and their relations with one another, we must seek to understand their work.
—Vollmer and Mills, *Professionalization.*

Although professions have existed for many years, the complex phenomena that we know today are reflections of twentieth-century, industrial society with its highly organized division of labor. As particular jobs and responsibilities became more organized and tasks more complex, the need for increased expertise in particular areas became essential. The specific characteristics or criteria of a twentieth-century profession reflect those needs: specialized skill and training; rules and norms of conduct (including ethics codes); minimum fees and salaries; formation of professional associations to govern practice; and qualifications for entrance to the profession.[2] Inherent in all the definitions is the underlying need for formal education and the exchange of critical knowledge. This essential exchange includes values and skills specific to each professional group and endorsement and support of established members within the profession.

The process of becoming a member of a profession has been referred to as *professionalization,* a dynamic process involving both *socialization* (the process of becoming adapted to the common needs or expectations of the group) and *acculturation* (the transfer of a culture from one group to another). Professionalization historically has referred to two separate operations: (1) the process by which various occupations achieve professional status; and (2) the process of training individuals for membership in a profession. The operation involving the training of individuals is of concern here.

Moral Direction of Professions

The underpinnings of any profession involve rules, expectations, and guidelines for appropriate or acceptable behavior. These frequently are referred to as principles of practice, codes of ethics, or moral imperatives. Imparting this "collective consciousness"[3] is essential in developing group membership and maintaining group values and ethics; all of these should be developed by the very group to which they apply.[4] One could discuss at length the fine delineation between values and ethics. As described in chapter 1, however, the determination used here is that values become operationalized in ethics or principles of practice, that such principles designed to govern practice reflect the underlying value scheme of the profession. It also is presumed that values are "one chief link binding members of a profession together. Professional values imply a consistent choice prevailing, it is claimed, over the lesser values of income, power, and prestige. Serious departure from these values carries with it the threat of excommunication."[5]

Ethics tell us what is right or wrong; values tell us what is preferred. Preference, in this case, dictates rules of ongoing behavior. Ethical behavior is not the decision between right and wrong in times of crisis; rather, it is the ongoing, ever-present demeanor reflective of one's underlying commitment.[6] Thus, codes of ethics should permeate all one's behavioral patterns.

MacIver said one of the key characteristics of a professional group was the degree to which its members established autonomy and collective self-control over their standards of performance and behavior.[7] He noted that professional ethics are not inviolate rules or commandments but, rather, spell out what is preferred or acceptable to the profession (universal good) and supply guidance in that direction. Professional ethics also provide grounds for professional sanction for those not respecting the profession's moral underpinnings. Lewis supports this author's contention by indicating that "professionals believe that practice should be moral; and to assure a moral practice, guidance needs to be provided to the practitioner."[8] Thus, codes of ethics specifically provide that guidance by spelling out what should or should not be done. This stance certainly appears to have been enhanced by the aftermath of Watergate, the more recent insider trading scandals on Wall Street, the increase in medical malpractice suits, and the increase in P.L. 94–142 hearings.[9] Involved, too, is the rise in professional accountability and consumer awareness, as evidenced in the preceding, as well as in recent child abuse cases questioning the role of professionals in appropriate detection and reporting procedures. The very fact that NASW recently has published a book about professional vulnerability[10] reinforces the importance of proper (that is, ethical) behavior and the potential vulnerability of those expected to exhibit it.

Influence of Professional Codes of Ethics

It is essential to have a basic understanding of the professional codes governing the practice and behavior of members of the professions examined here: social work, medicine, nursing, law, business, clinical psychology, and education. Each has several vehicles for guiding and monitoring the delivery of service and for assuring that professional values and standards are maintained. For the most part, adherence to the codes of ethics is tied to membership in the major professional organization.

NASW is the major organization for social work, and its underlying values and behavioral expectations are delineated in the NASW *Code of Ethics*.[11] The major tenets of the code emphasize the content of the four value scales included in POS: (1) respect for basic rights, (2) sense of social responsibility, (3) commitment to individual freedom, and (4) support of self-determination. SECTION VI of the code, entitled "The Social Worker's Ethical Responsibility to Society," highlights practice based on respect for basic rights (PARTS 1 and 2) as well as a strong sense of social responsibility (PARTS 6 and 7). SECTION VI also emphasizes commitment to individual freedom (PARTS 3 and 4). SECTION II, PART G, demands effort by social workers to foster maximum self-determination on the part of clients.

The American Medical Association (AMA) is the major professional organization for physicans. The preamble of the AMA *Principles of Medical Ethics* states:

> The medical profession has long subscribed to a body of ethical statements developed primarily for the benefit of the patient. As a member of this profession, a physician must recognize responsibility not only to patients, but also to society, to other health professionals, and to self. The following principles adopted by the American Medical Association are not laws, but standards of conduct which define the essentials of honorable behavior for the physician.[12]

Upon closer examination, Principle I, "A Physician shall be dedicated to providing competent medical service with compassion and respect for human dignity," appears to offer support for value 1 (respect for basic rights). Principle VII, "A physician shall recognize a responsibility to participate in activities contributing to an improved community," appears to support value 2 (sense of social responsibility). Principle III, "A physician shall respect the law and also recognize a responsibility to seek changes in those requirements which are contrary to the best interests of the patient," can be interpreted as being reflective of value 3 (commitment to individual freedom). Principle IV, "A physician shall respect the rights of patients, of colleagues, and of other health professionals, and shall safeguard patient confidences within the constraints of the law," appears to offer support for both value 3 (commitment to individual freedom) and value 4 (support of self-determination). No mention is made of respect for cultural, racial, or ethnic diversity. In fact, as is noted in Principle VI, "A physician shall, in the provision of appropriate patient care, except in emergencies, be free to choose whom to serve, with whom to associate, and the environment in which to provide medical services." It is hoped that emphasis of this latter principle is on "provision of appropriate care" and not on "free[dom] to choose whom to serve," which could encourage elements of disrespect and/or intolerance of diversity.

On a more optimistic note, it was encouraging to read a recent letter of acceptance to medical school that stated, "You have now taken the first step of your career in medicine and have therefore assumed certain responsibilities. Your personal and professional life must reflect the highest standards of moral integrity and professional dedication."[13] Perhaps the medical school will instill these values in the students during their next four years of school.

Members of the National Education Association (NEA) are expected to adhere to the *Code of Ethics of the Education Profession.* Its preamble states:

> The educator, believing in the worth and dignity of each human being, recognizes the supreme importance of the pursuit of truth, devotion to excellence, and the nurture of democratic principles. Essential to these goals is the protection of freedom to learn and to teach and the guarantee of equal educational opportunity for all. The educator accepts the responsibility to adhere to the highest ethical standards.[14]

The foregoing certainly supports the intent of value 1 (respect for basic rights); however, little emphasis appears to be directed toward value 2 (sense of social responsibility). Increased, although minimal, emphasis appears to be directed toward value 3 (commitment to individual freedom), as reflected in Principle I:

> [The educator] 3. shall not deliberately suppress or distort subject matter relevant to the student's progress; 4. shall make reasonable effort to protect the student from conditions harmful to learning or to health and safety; 5. shall not intentionally expose the student to embarrassment or disparagement.

Additional sections offer added support for value 1. Principle I states: "[The educator] 6. shall not on the basis of race, color, creed, sex, national origin, marital status, political or religious beliefs, family, social or cultural background, or sexual orientation, unfairly exclude . . . deny . . . grant advantage . . . to any student." Value 4 (support of self-determination) appears to be emphasized in Principle I: "[The educator] 1. shall not unreasonably restrain the student from independent action in the pursuit of learning and 2. shall not unreasonably deny the student access to varying points of view."

The ANA, in its *Code for Nurses,*[15] offers some overt support for the four social work values incorporated in POS. Item 1: "The nurse provides services with respect for human dignity and the uniqueness of the client unrestricted by considerations of social or economic status, personal attributes, or the nature of health problems," offers support for value 1 (respect for basic rights).

Items 7, 8, 10, and 11 appear to encourage a "sense of social responsibility" (value 2): "Item 7. The nurse participates in activities that contribute to the ongoing development of the profession's body of knowledge. Item 8.

The nurse participates in the profession's efforts to implement and improve standards of nursing....Item 10. The nurse participates in the profession's effort to protect the public from misinformation and misrepresentation and to maintain the integrity of nursing. Item 11. The nurse collaborates with members of the health professions and other citizens in promoting community and national efforts to meet the health needs of the public."

Value 3 (commitment to individual freedom) appears to be given attention in Item 2: "The nurse safeguards the client's right to privacy by judiciously protecting information of a confidential nature." Little emphasis appears to be placed on value 4 (support of self-determination), and no attention is given to the input of patients in relation to their own treatment plans. If stretched, however, item 1, with its emphasis on respect for human dignity, could be construed as offering some support for value 4.

Members of ABA, the major professional organization for lawyers, are guided by the *Model Code of Professional Responsibility*.[16] This code, made up of a series of canons, ethical considerations, and disciplinary rules, sets a minimum level of conduct. Currently some states are in the process of replacing this code with the *Model Rules of Professional Conduct,* adopted by the ABA House of Delegates on August 2, 1983.[17] The rules appear to be more socially responsible in some areas while being more restrictive in other areas.[18] Because the majority of states continue to rely on the *Model Code of Professional Responsibility* to guide behavior, it is that document which will be examined in light of the four primary social work values measured by POS.

The preamble of the ABA *Model Code* stresses respect for basic rights (value 1):

> The continued existence of a free and democratic society depends upon recognition of the concept that justice is based upon the rule of law grounded in respect for the dignity of the individual and his capacity through reason for enlightened self-government. Law so grounded makes justice possible, for only through such law does dignity of the individual attain respect and protection. Without it, individual rights become subject to unrestrained power, respect for law is destroyed, and rational self-government is impossible.

Value 3 (commitment to individual freedom) also is evident in that statement from the preamble.

Concern with value 2 (sense of social responsibility) appears in CANON 2 of the code: "A lawyer should assist the legal profession in fulfilling its duty to make legal counsel available." This is further elaborated by ethical considerations (ECs) 2-24 and 2-25, which follow from the basic canon. EC2-24 states:

> A layman whose financial ability is not sufficient to permit payment of any legal fee cannot obtain legal services, other than in cases where a contingent fee is

appropriate, unless the services are provided for him. Even a person of moderate means may be unable to pay a reasonable fee which is large because of the complexity, novelty, or difficulty of the problem or similar factors.

And EC2-25 goes on:

> Historically, the need for legal services of those unable to pay reasonable fees has been met in part by lawyers who donated their services or accepted court appointments on behalf of such individuals. The basic responsibility for providing legal services rests upon the individual lawyer, and personal involvement in the problems of the disadvantaged can be one of the most rewarding experiences in the life of a lawyer. Every lawyer, regardless of professional prominence or professional workload, should find time to participate in serving the disadvantaged. The rendition of free legal services to those unable to pay reasonable fees continues to be an obligation of each lawyer, but the efforts of individual lawyers are often not enough to meet the need. Thus it has been necessary for the profession to institute additional programs to provide legal services. Accordingly, legal aid offices, lawyer referral services, and other related programs have been developed, and others will be developed, by the profession.

Value 3 (commitment to individual freedom) is reflected in CANON 4: "A lawyer should preserve the confidences and secrets of a client," the ethical considerations of which spell out the details of expected performance. Value 3 also is supported by CANON 7: "A lawyer should represent a client zealously within the bounds of the law." EC7-12, in particular, outlines the need for advocacy in cases in which a mental or physical condition renders the client incapable. Other ethical considerations under CANON 7 clearly delineate behavior designed to assure maximum rights, freedom, and legal representation of all clients. CANON 7 also includes several ethical considerations that highlight support of self-determination (value 4). EC7-7 states:

> In certain areas of legal representation not affecting the merits of the cause or substantially prejudicing the rights of a client, a lawyer is entitled to make decisions on his own. But otherwise, the authority to make decisions is exclusively that of the client and, if made within the framework of the law, such decisions are binding on the lawyer.

EC7-8 states:

> A lawyer should exert his best efforts to insure that decisions of his client are made only after the client has been informed of relevant considerations. A lawyer ought to initiate this decision-making process if the client does not do so. Advice of a lawyer to his client need not be confined to purely legal considerations. A lawyer should advise his client of the possible effect of each legal alternative. The lawyer should bring to bear upon this decision-making process the fullness of his experience as well as his objective viewpoint.

This offers support of both value 4 (support of self-determination) and value 3 (commitment to individual freedom).

Note that the *Model Rules for Professional Conduct* place universal emphasis on pro bono (free) public service, whereas the more universally adopted *Model Code* puts that responsibility on the individual lawyer. In addition, since 1974, all law students have been required to take a course in professional responsibility designed to address common ethical dilemmas and the interpretation of various ethical aspects of the *Model Code*.

Business is represented by a number of major professional organizations, including the American Institute of Certified Public Accountants, the Society for the Advancement of Management, and the American Management Association. Because more than 50 percent of the businesspeople participating in this project belonged to the American Management Association, it seemed appropriate to focus on that organization's ethical code. It was surprising to discover that the organization does not have a code of ethics. The organization strongly states, however:

> We believe that management is the effective coordination and utilization of human effort and material resources to create and advance social values and community welfare. This capability should appear in all organizations—profit and nonprofit, private and public—and as such as a common denominator from which each may benefit. The process of management operates within a framework of moral forces which include: the dignity and value of the individual, the dignity of work, the dignity and validity of the profit motive, and the responsible exercise and control of power.[19]

It should be noted that the American Management Association takes no position on any public issue, speaks for no group, and espouses no cause other than better management. The foregoing certainly appears to foster respect for basic rights (value 1); however, no specific attention appears to be directed to the other three values.

The ethical principles of psychology are reflected in the American Psychological Association (APA) "Ethical Principles of Psychologists."[20] Respect for basic rights (value 1) is emphasized in the very first sentence of the preamble: "Psychologists respect the dignity and worth of the individual and strive for the preservation and protection of fundamental human rights." In Principle 3b: "As employees or employers, psychologists do not engage in or condone practices that are inhumane or that result in illegal or unjustifiable actions. Such practices include, but are not limited to, those based on considerations of race, handicap, age, gender, sexual preference, religion, or national origin in hiring, promotion, or training," additional evidence in support of both basic rights (value 1) and commitment to individual freedom (value 3) is present.

Additional support of value 3 appears in 3c: "In their professional roles, psychologists avoid any action that will violate or diminish the legal and civil rights of clients or of others who may be affected by their actions," and throughout the entirety of Principle 5, entitled "Confidentiality."

Sense of social responsibility (value 2) is strongly evident in Principle 1f: "As practitioners, psychologists know that they bear a heavy social responsibility because their recommendations and professional actions may alter the lives of others. They are alert to personal, social, organizational, financial, or political situations and pressures that might lead to misuse of their influence."

Although major emphasis is placed on professional relationships (with members of other professions) throughout Principle 7, "Professional Relationships," no emphasis appears to be directed toward relationships with clients from the perspective of value 4 (support of self-determination). Throughout the detailed list of principles, respect for clients in the form of informed consent, respect for confidentiality, respect for human subjects in the context of research as well as use of proper caution in interpreting research results suggests solid respect for clients. No emphasis, however, was placed on clients' rights to influence decisions or to maintain primacy in suggesting treatment goals and alternatives.

Interestingly, members of APA lauded the sense of social responsibility evident on the part of NASW members during Delegate Assembly in 1984. They countered their praise, however, with comments on the "disorganization" surrounding NASW efforts. That APA devoted two full pages of the *APA Monitor* to a detailed accounting of NASW efforts[21] can be interpreted as support and approval of NASW's sense of social responsibility. That APA offered criticism also can be construed as support directed toward improving effectiveness.

Examination of the various codes and principles espoused by members of major professional organizations reveals differing degrees of emphasis on the four basic social work values measured by POS. The task at hand is a comparison of value orientation scores, as reflected in POS, presented by seasoned professionals who represent the following seven major professions: (1) social work, (2) medicine, (3) business, (4) law, (5) education, (6) psychology, and (7) nursing.

Degree of Membership in Professional Associations

It is assumed that members of the various professions are influenced by the codes and principles endorsed by them through membership in their respective professional associations. Of the respondents, 87 percent of the social workers indicated membership in NASW; 52 percent of the physicians reported membership in AMA; and 57 percent of the businesspeople, membership in the American Management Association. Of the lawyers, 81 percent were members of ABA; 65 percent of the educators, of NEA; 87 percent of the psychologists, of APA; and 72 percent of the nurses, of ANA.

Although not all belonged to a professional association, a comparison of responses of members and nonmembers revealed no significant differences between their value score means. Therefore, it was decided to analyze responses on the basis of professional category or type rather than solely on professional organization membership. A comparison of value scores suggested that professionals were influenced by the philosophy and values of their major professional organization whether or not they were bona fide members.

Glimpse at Beginners

To have a full understanding of differences among seasoned professionals, it is necessary to have a basic understanding of differences among beginning students and recent graduates in the various professional fields. Similar to the foci of preceding chapters, the thrust here is a comparison of the degree of concurrence with the four basic social work values as reflected in the responses to POS of members of the various professional groups. As noted in chapter 3, beginning social work students come to their profession with a greater degree of concurrence with social work values than do students in business, public policy, social science, nursing, medicine, law, and education. This may be the result of a variety of factors, the two most likely being the self-selection process and admission review procedures. Further examination revealed that among professional groups at the undergraduate level, a significant amount of the variance of scores for values 1, 2, and 4 could be explained by the influence of specific demographic variables: family income, geographic region of birth, current region of residence, religion, and age (Table A-15, appendix A). In other words, when the influence of these demographic variables was controlled, the significant variance of value scores based on professional type alone disappeared, suggesting that the demographic variables were much more important than profession in contributing to value score variance. None of the demographic variables examined appeared to account for significant degrees of variance with respect to value 3. This suggests that in value 3 variance, professional type plays a major role.

At the graduate level, a number of demographic variables (political philosophy, gender, and religion) explained a significant amount of variance in all four values. Other variables contributed significantly to variance in several of the value scales: region of birth, age, current region of residence, and rural-urban dimensions of current residence. Although all contributed significantly to value score variance, none of the variables, taken either singularly or in combination, was sufficient to account for the significant variance among the various groups of graduate students about to begin their professional educational careers (Table A-15, appendix A). With the graduate students, it appeared that selection of profession played a more important role in contributing to the variance of respondents' value scores than was the case with the undergraduate students.

Glimpse at Recent Graduates

As noted in chapter 4, with experience and increased professional socialization, the differences among the various professional groups identified at the start of their academic training appeared to have become more pronounced by the time of graduation, with the results appearing to support the role of education in the professional socialization process. An examination of the impact of various demographic variables revealed that several contributed significantly to differences in score variance among the groups of graduates from the professional degree programs, but none was sufficient to account for significant differences in score variance among the professional groups at either the graduate or the undergraduate levels (Table A-18, appendix A). For recent graduates, it appeared that choice of profession played a major role in contributing to differences in value scores among the various groups of respondents. Although demographic variables no doubt played a role in determining choice of profession, the influence of the profession itself seemed to assume greater importance once the graduates were members of it.

Seasoned Professionals

Obviously, becoming a professional is a gradual process. Students enter educational programs with a predisposition toward their chosen field; the self-selection and admission processes are helpful in identifying appropriate candidates. The professional educational programs enhance professional socialization; the role of experience and interaction with professional peers also expands and solidifies that initial socialization. In speaking on law, Lortie provides a good example of a nervous, beginning lawyer "who has much to learn before his self and daily round conjoin. He must learn skills, roles, and values; he must puzzle through many dilemmas before experience results in moral decisiveness.[22] Lortie attributed some of this state to legal education, which, he notes, provides students with no real cases, as do medicine, dentistry, education, and social work. His example, however, seems to reflect adequately the state of most recent graduates about to launch their professional careers.

The beginning graduate does need additional socialization, as would any traveler at the beginning of a fairly long and somewhat tedious journey. Once he or she becomes more familiar with the nuances of traveling and the expectations of a traveler, as he or she becomes more familiar with the expectations of the profession and, in turn, becomes more adept at fulfilling those expectations, the traveler then begins to become more entrenched in the profession itself.

Based on the preceding, it was anticipated that seasoned professionals, or those with 10 or more years of postdegree experience, would exhibit a greater degree of professional socialization than would either beginning students or recent graduates, as illustrated by greater concurrence with the value scales in POS, as reflected by their higher value scores. It also was anticipated that, based on the nature and content of POS, social workers would exhibit greater concurrence with the four values than would members of any of the other professions.

Sample

A random sample of 823 professionals representing seven major professions was procured from the pool of individuals having been graduated between 1971 and 1975 from three major, mid-Atlantic universities—one public, the others private. Response rates varied from 42 percent for nurses to 10 percent for physicians, with the other professions ranging from 25 to 30 percent. Both business and social work had a response rate of 30 percent.

An examination of differences among professions revealed that groups were not homogeneous in age; gender; political party affiliation; political activity level; religion; geographic region of birth (for example, Northeast or Midwest); current region of residence; characteristics of current region of residence (for example, rural or major metropolitan); or current family income (see Table A-19, appendix A, for a summary of χ^2 findings).

Physicians and lawyers tended to be younger than members of the other professions; more than 85 percent were under age 45. This may reflect the sample size (that is, a 10-percent response rate for physicians, 27 percent for lawyers) or the self-selection of respondents and not reflect the general population. Medicine, business, and law had twice as large a proportion of males as did the other professions. Social work, medicine, law, and psychology all reported 60 to 65 percent Democrats. Business, on the other hand, reported 10 percent more Republicans than any other group and almost 15 percent more in the "undeclared" political category. A larger percentage of businesspeople classified themselves as conservative than of any other group, followed closely by educators.

Of the social workers, 34 percent reported being Protestant and 24 percent Roman Catholic. Physicians reported 48 percent Jewish and 20 percent Protestant. Businesspeople reported the highest percentage of Roman Catholics (36 percent), while educators reported the largest percentage of Protestants (49 percent). A larger percentage (15 percent) of social workers reported being born in rural communities than did any other professional group. All the responding physicians reported living in the northeastern United States, while only 60 percent of the social workers reported similarly. More than half the physicians reported that they currently live in large

Table 8.
Mean POS Value Scores of Seasoned Professionals by Professional Type

Profession	n	Value 1	Value 2	Value 3	Value 4
Social work	384	43.63	38.16	33.54	43.81
Medicine[a]	25	43.08	34.52	29.04	42.68
Business	89	38.96	30.40	25.31	39.19
Law	81	42.23	34.88	31.13	41.73
Education	85	41.11	34.34	27.85	40.98
Psychology	76	44.18	37.22	31.51	44.36
Nursing	83	43.20	32.99	26.67	43.10
Total	823				
Mean		42.72	35.89	30.81	42.76

[a]Low rate of response.

metropolitan areas, whereas only 5 percent of responding educators live in similar circumstances. Current family income also differed by profession: all physicians reported an income exceeding $45,000, as did 83 percent of the businesspeople and 84 percent of the lawyers. In other categories, fewer than 50 percent reported that amount.

Additional information could be provided about the sample. However, only major differences are included to convey an overall picture of the various professional groups. None of the findings should evoke surprise except, perhaps, for the age of lawyers and physicians. Based on common knowledge, most of the differences could have been anticipated. What is critical is understanding how these differences impinge on professional values. The impact of the differences with respect to variability in value scores among professional groups is examined from several perspectives later.

Analysis of Value Score Differences

A comparison of value score means of the seasoned professionals, those with at least 10 years of postdegree experience (Table 8), reveals that significant differences continue to exist among the professional groups. Social workers scored higher than all other professionals on all the values except for values 1 and 4; for those two values, clinical psychologists scored about a half-point higher, a difference that was not by any means significant. Further statistical analyses revealed that members of the various professions do indeed exhibit different mean scores on the four values represented in POS. A summary of F scores and probability levels are presented in Table A-20, appendix A. Box-plots clearly illustrate the median and variance differences among the professional groups (Figure 7). Examination of the box-plots reveals that the responses of the various professionals seem to support

Figure 7.
Box-Plots for Value Scores of Seasoned Professionals

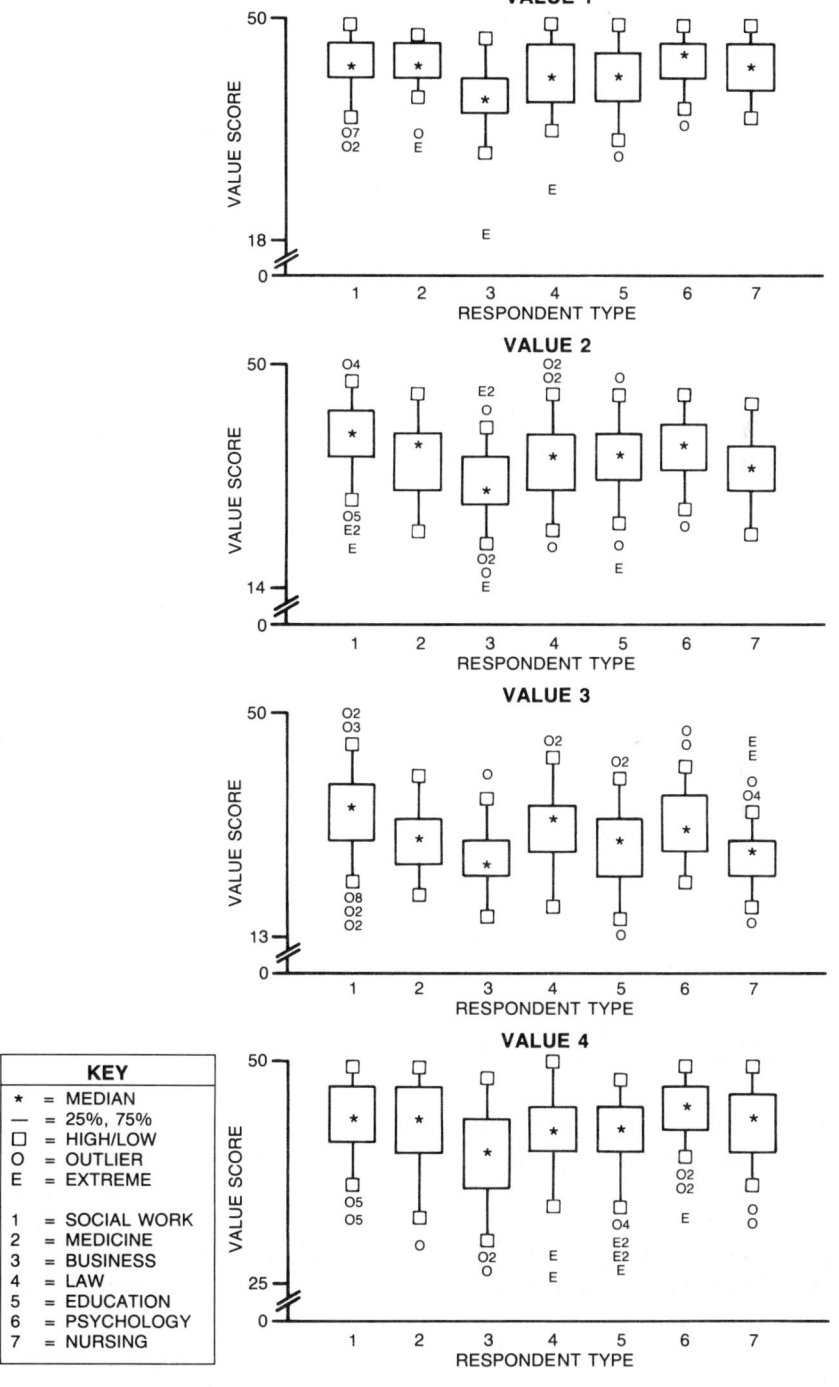

Table 9.
Significant Differences between Means of Social Workers and Other Seasoned Professionals Based on Tukey's Honestly Significant Difference

Profession Values:	Medicine				Business				Law				Education				Psychology				Nursing			
	1	2	3	4	1	2	3	4	1	2	3	4	1	2	3	4	1	2	3	4	1	2	3	4
Social work	*	*			*	*	*	*		*			*	*	*						*			*

$* = p < .05$ (values whose means differed significantly between designated groups).

a pattern that is repeated throughout the four value scales. For the most part, scores increase from the point of beginning professional education up to graduation, then decrease slightly from graduation to a point at least 10 years into professional practice.

A comparison of value score means using Tukey's Honestly Significant Difference revealed that social workers differed significantly from businesspeople on all four values, from educators on three out of four values, from nurses and physicians on two of the four values, and from lawyers on one value—value 2 (Table 9). Social workers and psychologists did not differ significantly on any value.

It is somewhat surprising that social workers differed from lawyers on value 2—sense of social responsibility. All lawyers, especially ABA members, must adhere to a *Model Code of Social Responsibility,* and all lawyers who began law school after 1974 were required to take a course in social responsibility, a requirement for program accreditation initiated by ABA, the same year. In comparing all lawyers ($n = 52$) with those who report membership in ABA ($n = 42$), no significant differences between the two categories were noted. In comparing physicians who were members of AMA with those who were not, it was interesting that members of AMA differed from members of NASW on all four values. Those physicians who were not members of AMA, however, differed from social workers on only two out of four values. Is it possible that physicians who decline membership in AMA are a less conservative breed? Could it be construed that, as a result, they are more liberal? More socially responsible? One must be cautious with such speculation considering the size of the sample on which such speculation is based. One must remember to offer proper respect and caution when using the term "speculation." On a firmer note, it is not surprising that social workers did not differ from clinical psychologists, considering the strong similarities between the codes governing the behavior of members of their respective professional organizations and the foci of their activities, especially in direct practice.

Examination of the influence of demographic variables on the variance of value scores among professionals revealed a number of variables that were significant. Inclusion of these variables, however, was insufficient to account for differences in variance of values scores among the professional groups. This held true for professions based primarily on undergraduate degrees as well as for those professions requiring graduate degrees (Table A-21, appendix A). Political party membership was by far the most important demographic, followed by religion, gender, age, and total family income. Types of clients served (for example, other professionals, middle-class workers, the working poor); type of major work setting (for example, publicly funded, privately financed); and number of years in the profession also were significant.

Socialization Process Over Time

Two major concerns have been how professions differ in their value orientations and how these differences vary with respect to relative time or point in professional career. A comparison of value scores for the various professions at differing times (at admission, on graduation, and after at least 10 years in the field) can be obtained by comparing Tables 2, 4, and 8. Table A-22 (appendix A) summarizes results of two-way analyses of variance based on profession and point in time. To facilitate comparisons, the contents of Tables 2, 4, and 8 have been consolidated into Tables 10, 11, 12, and 13. The data presented include mean value scores for each profession for each specific time period (at the beginning, at graduation, and at least 10 years after graduation).

Table 10.
ANOVAs of Value 1 Scores by Profession and Point in Professional Career

Profession	Beginning Students	Graduates	Seasoned Professionals
Undergraduate degree			
Social work	42.07	44.18	43.63
Education	40.45	42.72	41.11
Nursing	40.40	43.10	43.20
Business	38.81	40.27	38.96
Graduate degree			
Social work	42.75	44.13	43.63
Law	41.31	41.54	42.23
Business	40.73	40.21	38.96
Education	40.33	42.74	41.11
Medicine	39.62	41.58	43.08

Table 11.
ANOVAs of Value 2 Scores by Profession
and Point in Professional Career

Profession	Beginning Students	Graduates	Seasoned Professionals
Undergraduate degree			
Social work	36.90	39.35	38.16
Nursing	34.84	34.57	32.99
Education	34.36	34.84	34.34
Business	34.23	33.37	30.40
Graduate degree			
Social work	37.62	39.25	38.16
Education	34.56	34.57	34.34
Medicine	34.02	34.42	34.52
Law	33.35	32.62	34.88
Business	31.64	33.21	30.40

Data are presented separately for professions requiring advanced degrees and those requiring bachelor's degrees for professional entry. Data used earlier in this chapter were pooled for the two-way analyses of variance. Note that only those professions for which data for all three timeframes are available have been included. Clinical psychology, which was included in earlier analyses in this chapter, has been dropped from the current comparative material for that reason.

Table 12.
ANOVAs of Value 3 Scores by Profession
and Point in Professional Career

Profession	Beginning Students	Graduates	Seasoned Professionals
Undergraduate degree			
Social work	31.38	33.03	33.54
Education	25.86	26.68	27.85
Business	24.90	26.24	25.31
Nursing	24.12	27.43	26.67
Graduate degree			
Social work	30.66	33.20	33.54
Education	29.37	26.91	27.85
Medicine	28.82	26.08	29.04
Law	28.54	30.31	31.12
Business	22.70	26.28	25.31

Table 13.
ANOVAs of Value 4 Scores by Profession and Point in Professional Career

Profession	Beginning Students	Graduates	Seasoned Professionals
Undergraduate degree			
Nursing	42.84	44.62	43.10
Social work	42.31	43.88	43.81
Education	41.68	42.92	40.98
Business	39.69	41.12	39.19
Graduate degree			
Social work	43.21	43.81	43.81
Education	43.26	43.22	40.98
Law	41.67	41.31	41.73
Medicine	41.35	43.17	42.68
Business	40.16	41.05	39.19

Combined Impact of Professional Choice and Time

Results of the two-way analyses of variance (Table A-22, appendix A), based on professional type and particular time in professional career, revealed that, for the most part, profession and time contribute significantly to differences in value score variance. The influence of a particular time was usually the same for all professions. There was a beginning baseline measure for new students, a substantial increase in the scores of recent graduates, then a drop in the scores of seasoned professionals. Note that scores of seasoned business professionals seemed to drop more sharply than did those of other professionals. In a few instances—specifically, value 2 for professions based on undergraduate degrees and values 1 and 3 for professions requiring advanced degrees—the influence of time differed among the professions. For some professions, the scores of graduates were lower than those of beginning students, followed by an upswing in the scores of seasoned professionals; for others, scores followed a more consistent pattern.

Larger Picture

In examining value patterns over time, it is evident that after 10 or more years in the field, values of virtually all the professional groups tended to drop slightly, with business dropping more drastically. This simply may be the result of a general learning curve phenomenon—regression to the mean: after mastery of material, some is forgotten. Although there is some loss of initial mastery, the majority of material is retained.

Another possibility is that recent graduates and seasoned professionals are products of different times. Unfortunately, the data are not longitudinal. Ten or more years ago, professional values may not have been stressed to the extent they are today. In other words, recent graduates and seasoned professionals may not have had similar experiences. This may explain the dramatic drop in the value scores of seasoned business professionals. Although increased emphasis recently has been placed on business ethics, especially among students and budding professionals, the impact may not have filtered into the seasoned professional group yet. After all, many of the actions of that seasoned group are what prompted the initial increase in attention to values and ethics.

Speaking of students of the sixties in his recent book, *The Closing of the American Mind,* Allan Bloom indicates that they forced their own values to the forefront. Whether those values reflected basic values of the times remains an unanswered question. What was evident was that "the university had abandoned all claim to study or inform about value—undermining the sense of value of what it taught, while turning over the 'decision' about values to the folk, the 'Zeitgeist,' the relevant."[23] What traditionally has been assigned to students of the sixties was an external, beneficent focus espousing the well-being of others, rather than the internal, amoral, self-serving focus suggested by Bloom.

To give claim solely to the students and their control of the situation would be unfair. Although students may have been somewhat successful in their striving to run counter to general society, the opinions of the majority obviously had an impact. Tocqueville found "that Americans talked very much about individual rights but that there was a real monotony of thought and that vigorous independence of mind was rare," as reported in Bloom.[24] Robert B. Reich aptly describes this in his discussion of Ronald Reagan: "Reagan's success lay not in changing the nation's view of how the world works—he had been saying the same things for years, after all, without sparking much of a response—but in giving clear voice to themes the public had finally shown itself ready to embrace."[25] The public allowed Ronald Reagan to come into his own.

Up through the end of the Vietnam War and the war on poverty, the students of the sixties were in the midst of a society more willing to act in a socially responsible fashion, encouraging self-determination of the people. These students also experienced an economy more tolerant of financing such efforts. As the economy flattened and major efforts to quell inflation were instituted, the majority focus became more self-centered, less generous, and more controlling in its expectations of others. Other people, such as Bloom, might contend that the majority focus was self-serving from the start. This latter opinion certainly offers apt support for the lower scores of today's seasoned professionals or, as might be noted, the former students of the sixties.

According to current thought, it is not surprising that business has the lowest profile in a value domain populated by such principles as redistribution of wealth.[26] What is surprising is the severe drop in value scores of businesspeople following graduation, especially considering the recent attention given to business ethics.[27] As previously noted, this may be because the data are not longitudinal and not because of a change in value orientation. Also, ethics may not have been stressed as much in earlier times.

Considering the value hierarchy proposed for the four values addressed by POS and the fact that most professional ethics codes cited earlier support these two values, it is somewhat surprising that the scores of the various professions were not more similar on values 1 and 2. Instead, the findings suggest that whether or not a value hierarchy in fact does exist, social workers exhibit the greatest concurrence with all four values regardless of the particular time in their professional careers. Of course, one could contend that giving lip service to a code is not the same as stressing specific values throughout professional socialization and on an ongoing basis in the publications and meetings of the major professional association. Note again that in some cases, even the content of the codes of ethics does not refer to the four basic values. For example, the code of the NEA does not mention "sense of social responsibility," nor do the codes of the APA or ANA appear to mention "support of self-determination." The American Management Association, lacking a code, overlooks all but "respect for basic rights."

Additional examination of respondents consisting solely of the social work categories indicates that there are no significant differences between the means of beginning students, recent graduates, seasoned professionals, social work faculty, and field instructors. The only difference was that noted earlier in chapter 3 between beginning students and social work faculty, a difference that had disappeared by graduation. The bottom line is that seasoned social workers scored higher than members of any other profession.

The same general patterning existed when the other professions were compared along the dimension of time or point in one's career. This suggests that although value score changes were noted between points in time, the professions tended to exhibit similar patterns of change over time except for those in business, whose scores dropped more dramatically and rapidly. As noted previously, this drop may be due to the fact that different groups of business professionals (beginning students, recent graduates, and seasoned professionals) were trained at different times. Examination of data on members of all professions revealed that members of each specific profession tended to hover around a general score. Thus, the contention that professions do indeed differ in their overall value orientation is supported, at least as reflected in their degree of concurrence with the four social work values, as measured by POS. Greater concurrence with the espoused values is reflected in higher scores on POS.

In examining the contents of Tables 10, 11, 12, and 13, one can determine which professions are more similar with respect to each value. For example, on most values, social workers are more like educators and less like businesspeople. As noted earlier, however, although scores may be closer together between education and social work, the value means of the two professions remain significantly different on three out of four values. These findings support those of some earlier researchers. Kidneigh and Lundberg found social workers and educators to be similar on certain dimensions, yet different on others.[28] McLeod and Meyer found them to differ on six out of nine basic social work values.[29] While noting major differences between social work and business students, Feld and Marks opened another area for examination: the differences between social workers involved in direct practice and those in administration.[30] Those in administration appear to be more similar to businesspeople, at least in their perceptions of power. Such differences are explored more fully in chapter 7.

In summary, the data presented here show that members of the various professions do indeed have different value preferences. Social workers present the strongest degree of concurrence with the four values in POS, followed by members of the other professions. It was anticipated that social workers would score higher. It was surprising, however, that—based on the content of various professional codes of ethics—there was not more similarity in value scores among the professions, especially on value 1, because it was mentioned in all the codes. Patterns of change over time appear to be similar among the professions, with little change in pattern noted among the various professions. Degrees of difference among professions that existed at the beginning of careers continued to be evident at graduation and well into years of professional practice. Even though social work focused on professional socialization as related to values, all other professions appear to do the same, based on the consistent pattern of value change among them.

In general, although the demographic variables appear to have an impact on value variance, that impact was insufficient for the specific variables to be considered more influential than professional affiliation. Professional type seemed to be the divider in explaining variance of value scores. This finding is examined in greater detail in chapter 6.

Notes and References

1. H. M. Vollmer and D. L. Mills, eds., *Professionalization* (Englewood Cliffs, N.J.: Prentice-Hall, 1966), p. v.

2. *For an overview, see* A. M. Carr-Saunders and P. A. Wilson, *The Professions* (Oxford, England: Clarendon Press, 1933); A. Etzioni, *Semi-Professions and Their Organizations* (New York: Free Press, 1969); and A. Flexner, "Is Social Work a Profession?" *Proceedings of the National*

Conference of Charities and Correction (Chicago: Hildman Printing Co., 1915).

3. E. Durkheim, *Education and Society,* S. D. Fox, trans. (Glencoe, Ill.: Free Press, 1956), p. 70.

4. E. Durkheim, *Professional Ethics and Civic Morals,* C. Brookfield, trans. (Glencoe, Ill.: Free Press, 1958).

5. R. H. Jones, "Social Values and Social Work Education," in K. A. Kendall, ed., *Social Work Values in an Age of Discontent* (New York: Council on Social Work Education, 1970), p. 39.

6. M. Levine, "Nursing Ethics and the Ethical Nurse," *American Journal of Nursing,* 77 (May 1977), p. 846.

7. R. M. MacIver, "The Social Significance of Professional Ethics," *Annals of the American Academy of Political and Social Science,* 297 (January 1955), pp. 118–124.

8. H. Lewis, *The Intellectual Base of Social Work Practice* (New York: Lois & Samuel Silberman Fund, 1982), p. 83.

9. *Public Law 94-142, Education for All Handicapped Act (1975),* federally mandated education for all handicapped students between ages 3 and 21. This law gave parents the right to question the appropriateness of their child's educational plan; it also gave educators the responsibility of providing the best educational plan for each child.

10. D. J. Besharov, *The Vulnerable Social Worker: Liability for Serving Children and Families* (Silver Spring, Md.: National Association of Social Workers, Inc., 1985).

11. *Code of Ethics* (Washington, D.C.: National Association of Social Workers, Inc., 1980).

12. "Principles of Medical Ethics," as contained in the *Current Opinions of the Council on Ethical and Judicial Affairs of the American Medical Association* (Chicago: American Medical Association, 1986), p. ix.

13. Excerpt from a personal acceptance letter (dated June 18, 1987) to a prospective medical student from Dean J. A. Dieterle, Philadelphia College of Osteopathic Medicine.

14. "Code of Ethics of the Education Profession," in *NEA Handbook, 1986-87* (Washington, D.C.: National Education Association, 1986), pp. 288–289.

15. *Code for Nurses* (Kansas City, Mo.: American Nurses Association, 1976).

16. *Model Code of Professional Responsibility* (Chicago: American Bar Association, 1981).

17. *Model Rules of Professional Conduct* (Chicago: American Bar Association, 1983).

18. *For a detailed comparison of the* Model Code of Professional Responsibility *and the* Model Rules of Professional Conduct, *see* T. D. Morgan and R. D. Rotunda, *1987 Selected Standards on Professional Responsibility*

(Mineola, N.Y.: Foundation Press, 1987), pp. 189–204.

19. This quote comes from an undated reprint sent to the author from the American Management Association in July 1987.

20. American Psychological Association, "Ethical Principles of Psychologists," *American Psychologist,* 36 (June 1981), pp. 633–638. This version was adopted by the APA Council of Representatives on January 24, 1981.

21. S. Cunningham, "NASW Across-the-Board Political Activism Reflects Diversity of Membership," *American Psychological Association Monitor,* 16 (April 1985), pp. 8–9.

22. D. C. Lortie, "Layman to Lawman: Law School, Careers, and Professional Socialization," *Harvard Educational Review,* 29 (Fall 1959), p. 363.

23. A. Bloom, *The Closing of the American Mind: How Education Has Failed Democracy and Impoverished the Souls of Today's Students* (New York: Simon & Schuster, 1987), pp. 313–314.

24. Ibid., p. 247.

25. R. B. Reich, *Tales of a New America* (New York: Times Books, 1987), p. 21.

26. Bloom, *The Closing of the American Mind,* p. 370.

27. S. Dentzer and M. Malone, "M.B.A.'s Learn a Human Touch," *Newsweek,* June 16, 1986, pp. 48–50.

28. J. C. Kidneigh and H. W. Lundberg, "Are Social Work Students Different?" *Social Work,* 3 (July 1958), pp. 57–61.

29. D. L. McLeod and H. J. Meyer, "A Study of the Values of Social Workers," in E. J. Thomas, ed., *Behavioral Science for Social Workers* (New York: Free Press, 1967), pp. 401–416.

30. A. Feld and R. Marks, "Self-Perceptions of Power: Do Social Work and Business Students Differ?" *Social Work,* 32 (May–June 1987), pp. 225–230.

S·I·X

Demographics:
Political Philosophy, Geography, Social Class, Religion, Gender, and Age

◆

Throughout chapters 1 through 5, the findings have indicated that professional type has contributed significantly to value score differences. In all cases, the value scores of social workers were significantly different from those of businesspeople. In many cases, the scores of social workers differed significantly from those of physicians, lawyers, educators, and nurses. In examining the influence of specific demographic variables on value score variance, many covariates were found to be significant, including political philosophy, gender, religion, age, political activity level, political party membership, family income, current residence, birthplace, type of clients served, and type of employment (public; private, nonprofit; and private, for-profit). The focus of this chapter is on the variables that are the most important contributors to variability in value scores. Is profession the most important contributor, or do other factors contribute more heavily? If so, which ones?

The literature suggests that professions do differ in their overall value orientations, an idea supported by the findings reported in earlier chapters.[1] The literature also supports the importance of specific demographic variables. For example, James noted the importance of types of clients served.[2] She found that those professionals who worked with welfare clients were more sympathetic toward them; those who did not were less sympathetic and less respectful. James also found similarities and differences in views toward poverty based on personal experiences and outlooks among the various professionals. Grimm and Orten found age; marital status; parenthood (or its absence); SES; geographic region of residence; and professional experience to play significant roles in attitudes toward the poor.[3] McLeod and Meyer found that religion had a significant impact on values; professed Protestants and Roman Catholics scored lower on various values than did Jews and people reporting no religious affiliation.[4] As noted in previous chapters, McLeod and Meyer also found the amount of education

---

In the context of a calling, to enter a profession meant to take up a definite function in a community and to operate within the civic and civil order of that community. The profession as career was no longer oriented to any face-to-face community but to impersonal standards of excellence, operating in the context of a national occupational system. Rather than embedding one in a community, following a profession came to mean, quite literally, "to move up and away."
—R. N. Bellah et al., *Habits of the Heart*
(New York: Harper & Row, 1985), pp. 119–120.

---

to have a positive impact on value scores. The higher the educational level, the more positive the value scores. Cryns, on the other hand, found that graduate students, with their increased amount of education, had more negative attitudes toward human nature scales than did undergraduates.[5] Cryns specifically noted that previous work experience did not significantly influence attitude differences with respect to views of human nature; however, he mentioned both gender and, as previously noted, academic status as having a significant impact. Cryns noted that both gender and education (academic status) also were important with respect to views toward poverty. Graduate students attributed less prominence to a fatalistic interpretation of cause and placed more responsibility on the individual person, a tendency that applied only to males. With respect to the opposite end of the financial spectrum, economic success, the impact of both gender and education was similar.

Varley reported that SES influenced value scores.[6] She noted that political philosophy, region of residence, age, gender, and prior work experience also contributed significantly to value score variance. Those subjects who were identified as being more politically liberal scored higher on specific value scales. Those subjects residing in the Northeast and those in administrative positions also scored higher on specific value scales. Younger people had a tendency to score higher, as did males. Prior work experience tended to have a negative effect on value change; students with prior work experience scored in the middle ranks on some values and in the lowest ranks on others.

Identifying the Influence of Demographic Variables

Which variables have the greatest impact on value score variance? In this chapter, the influence of previously identified demographic variables is examined together with the influence of professional type. Subjects included 1,890 professionals representing seven major professions: (1) social work, (2) medicine, (3) business, (4) law, (5) education, (6) clinical psychology, and (7) nursing. Basic demographic information about the subjects is illustrated in Table 14.

Description of the Professionals

By intent, social workers made up the largest category, followed by business. Over one-third of all subjects were between the ages of 36 and 45. Close to 65 percent were female; only 13 percent were minorities. More than half were married, and almost one-third were single; fewer than one-tenth were divorced. More than 40 percent were childless; more than 33 percent had two to three children. Almost 50 percent were registered Democrats; over 20 percent were independents. Slightly fewer than 50 percent referred to themselves as politically moderate. Close to one-third were identified as politically liberal. Almost 68 percent described themselves as voting in most elections and as closely following issues. Fourteen percent indicated that they sometimes vote in major elections.

Each subject received scores on the four value scales of POS plus a total value score. For the most part, data were interval level; for some variables, the data were ordinal level but could be translated easily to interval level. Several variables, by their very nature, had to be coded as dummy variables (that is, presence versus absence): race, marital status, political party affiliation, religious affiliation, birthplace, current region of residence, and profession. Data were analyzed by means of stepwise multiple regressions.[7] Predictive models for POS total value, value 1, value 2, value 3, and value 4 scores were obtained by means of five separate regression equations. The independent variables included profession; age; gender; race; marital status; political party affiliation; political philosophy; political activity level; religious affiliation; birthplace; characteristics of birthplace (for example, rural versus urban); current region of residence; characteristics of current residence; current family income; SES based on father's educational level; characteristics of major work setting (private, nonprofit; public, nonprofit; and private, for-profit); and number of years in the profession.

Almost one-third of the various professionals reported being Jewish and slightly less than one-third, Protestant. More than 18 percent reported they were Roman Catholic. Almost three-fourths were born in the northeastern United States. Characteristics of birthplace covered the gamut from rural to large metropolitan areas. Currently, almost 84 percent live in the Northeast.

Table 14.
Specific Sample Characteristics (n = 1,890)

Demographic Variable	n	%	Demographic Variable	n	%
Profession			Other	25	1.3
Social work	947	50.1	None	210	11.1
Medicine	102	5.4	Missing	28	1.5
Business	265	14.0	Political philosophy		
Law	189	10.0	Conservative	211	11.7
Education	182	9.6	Moderate	928	49.1
Clinical psychology	76	4.0	Liberal	607	32.1
Nursing	129	6.8	Other	98	5.2
Age			Missing	36	1.9
Under 25	325	17.2	Political activity level		
26–35	435	23.0	Disinterested,		
36–45	721	38.1	uninvolved	91	4.8
46–55	250	13.2	Sometimes vote	266	14.1
Over 55	145	7.7	Vote, follow issues		
Missing	14	0.7	closely	1,283	67.9
Gender			Support issues,		
Male	636	33.7	candidates	168	8.9
Female	1,228	64.9	Run for office, money		
Missing	26	1.4	to candidates	62	3.3
Race			Missing	20	1.1
Black	134	7.1	Religion		
White (Caucasian)	1,646	87.1	Jewish	349	18.5
Hispanic	39	2.1	Protestant	517	27.4
Other	47	2.5	Roman Catholic	607	32.1
Missing	24	1.3	Other	116	6.2
Marital status			None	268	14.2
Single	577	30.5	Missing	33	1.7
Married	1,033	54.7	Birthplace		
Divorced	179	9.5	Northeast	1,410	74.6
Widowed	33	1.7	South	119	6.3
Other	47	2.5	Midwest	182	9.6
Missing	21	1.1	West	41	2.2
Number of children			Outside USA	107	5.7
None	816	43.2	Missing	31	1.6
1	264	13.9	Characteristics of birthplace		
2–3	675	35.7	Rural	149	7.9
4–5	96	5.1	Small town (less than		
More than 5	25	1.3	100,000)	454	24.0
Missing	14	0.7	Mid-sized		
Political party affiliation			(100,000–500,000)	353	18.7
Republican	308	16.3	Suburban (outside		
Democrat	925	48.9	major metropolitan		
Independent	394	20.8	area	336	17.8

Table 14. (Continued)

Demographic Variable	n	%	Demographic Variable	n	%
Metropolitan (more than 500,000)	570	30.2	Current family income		
			Less than $14,999	116	6.1
Missing	28	1.5	$15,000–19,999	134	7.1
Current residence			$20,000–29,999	245	12.9
Northeast	1,585	83.9	$30,000–44,999	492	26.0
South	79	4.2	More than $45,000	856	45.3
Midwest	82	4.3	Missing	47	2.5
West	95	5.0	Father's educational level		
Outside USA	11	0.6	Eight or fewer years	279	14.8
Missing	38	2.0	Some high school	229	12.1
Characteristics of residence			High school graduation	655	35.2
Rural	131	6.9	College graduation	332	17.6
Small town (less than 100,000)	580	30.7	Postbaccalaureate	365	19.3
			Missing	30	1.6
Mid-sized (100,000–500,000)	266	14.1	Mother's educational level		
			Eight or fewer years	210	11.1
Suburban (outside major metropolitan area)	614	32.5	Some high school	230	12.2
			High school graduation	880	46.6
			College graduation	355	17.7
Metropolitan (more than 500,000)	263	13.9	Postbaccalaureate	178	9.4
			Missing	37	1.9
Missing	36	1.9			

Again, characteristics of current residence cover a wide range in population size. More than 45 percent of the subjects reported family incomes exceeding $45,000; 26 percent reported incomes between $30,000 and $45,000; and 13 percent reported incomes under $20,000. Fathers' and mothers' educational levels were similar, with 35 percent of fathers and almost 47 percent of mothers being high school graduates. Almost 37 percent of fathers were college graduates or had advanced degrees; 27 percent of mothers had college degrees.

Two extremes should be noted: specifically, the large percentage of subjects born in the Northeast and the large number currently living in the same area. This most likely was due to the fact that the three major universities from which subjects were procured were located in that part of the country. Subjects included beginning students, graduates, and alumni from these schools plus a national random sample of NASW members. The subjects included represent a composite of those involved in chapters 3, 4, and 5, plus an additional 131 who returned their completed scales too late for inclusion in earlier chapters.

Demographics

Additional examination of the data for each profession indicates similarities in variable distribution among the various professions. The data for the specific professions are not reported here because of those similarities. What is essential is that the data seem to reflect general attributes of the larger professional population.

Stepwise multiple regression, as a mathematical operation, develops a representative model of the influence of each independent variable on the dependent variable. The model selected here illustrates, by descending stepwise order, the variables that explain the greatest amount of variance in the dependent variable. If a variable does not contribute significantly to a reduction of the residual or unexplained variance, it is not included in the equation. To determine a greater understanding of the relationships among the various demographic variables, and to determine which variables to include in the stepwise regression, correlation coefficients were examined. Most correlations between variables were less than 0.1; a few variables were more highly correlated (Table A-23, appendix A). These latter relationships were not surprising; rather, they supported the quality of the data. For example, it was expected that a high negative correlation would exist between age and single marital status: the older one is, the less likely one is to be single. In other words, as age increases, the likelihood of single status decreases. On the other hand, one would expect that as age increases, the likelihood of married marital status increases. Thus, a high positive correlation exists between the two variables.

It is not surprising that a negative correlation existed between age of subjects and parents' educational level or that a high positive correlation was found between parents' educational levels. As the general population becomes more educated, the likelihood increases of younger people having more highly educated parents than their older peers. It is also quite reasonable to assume that people marry people with similar educational backgrounds—thus, the high positive correlation between parents' educational levels.

Additional correlations suggest that people are likely to remain in the same part of the country where they were born. The correlations also suggest that reported Republicans have a more conservative political philosophy and report being less politically active than do their Democratic counterparts.

In Table 15 is a summary of the stepwise selection of the independent variables as they relate to the five dependent variables. A summary of the variables, their order of selection, and the proportional reduction of unexplained variance by each variable (r^2 change) are presented. Additionally, reported in Table 15 are the variables selected in relation to total value scores first, followed by those additional variables selected by each independent value scale.

Table 15.
Variables Selected by Stepwise Multiple Regression
for Predicting Value Scale Scores

Variables	Order Selected	r^2	r^2 change
Total Value Score			
Political philosophy	1	.19274	.19274
Social work professional	2	.31334	.12060
Democrat	3	.35374	.04040
Business professional	4	.36920	.01546
Independent politics	5	.37773	.00853
Nontraditional religion	6	.38533	.00760
Psychology professional	7	.39022	.00489
Other races[a]	8	.39380	.00358
Political activity level	9	.39730	.00350
Gender	10	.40099	.00349
Current family income	11	.40417	.00318
Character of current residence	12	.40723	.00306
Nontraditional politics	13	.41009	.00286
Divorced	14	.41201	.00192
Black	15	.41392	.00191
Current residence in Northeast	16	.41506	.00114
Current residence in South	17	.41430	.00076
Value 1			
Political philosophy	2	.09608	.03735
Social work professional	1	.05873	.05873
Democrat	4	.12905	.01519
Business professional	5	.14141	.01236
Independent politics			
Nontraditional religion			
Psychology professional	6	.14712	.00571
Race/nonblack, white, Hispanic			
Political activity level	9	.16292	.00460
Gender	14	.17642	.00199
Current family income			
Character of current residence	13	.17443	.00208
Nontraditional politics			
Divorced			
Black			
Current residence in Northeast	7	.15277	.00565
Current residence in South			
Variables not selected by total value score:			
White	3	.11386	.01778
Nursing professional	8	.15837	.00560
Republican	10	.16630	.00338
Roman Catholic	11	.16950	.00320
Protestant	12	.17235	.00285

Table 15. (Continued)

Variables	Order Selected	r^2	r^2 change
Value 2			
Political philosophy	1	.16893	.16893
Social work professional	2	.26261	.09368
Democrat	3	.30248	.03987
Business professional	12	.33201	.00154
Independent politics			
Nontraditional religion			
Psychology professional	7	.32142	.00295
Other races			
Political activity level	11	.33047	.00171
Gender			
Current family income	5	.31513	.00502
Character of current residence			
Nontraditional politics			
Divorced			
Black	10	.32876	.00180
Current residence in Northeast			
Current residence in South	6	.31847	.00334
Variables not selected by total value scores			
White			
Nursing professional			
Republican	4	.31011	.00763
Roman Catholic			
Protestant			
Jewish	8	.32420	.00278
Character of birthplace	9	.32696	.00276
Law professional	13	.33335	.00134

Variables	Order Selected	r^2	r^2 change
Value 3			
Political philosophy	1	.15357	.15357
Social work professional	2	.25796	.10439
Democrat	3	.29655	.03859
Business professional	5	.31545	.00879
Independent politics	6	.32215	.00670
Nontraditional religion	7	.32655	.00440
Psychology professional			
Other races			
Political activity level	8	.33017	.00362
Gender			
Current family income			
Character of current residence	9	.33367	.00350
Nontraditional politics	10	.33631	.00264
Divorced			
Black			
Current residence in Northeast			
Current residence in South			

Table 15. (Continued)

Variables	Order Selected	r^2	r^2 change
Variables not selected by total value score:			
White	13	.34385	.00233
Nursing professional	11	.33893	.00262
Republican			
Roman Catholic			
Protestant			
Jewish	15	.34671	.00127
Character of birthplace			
Law professional			
Age	4	.30666	.01011
Married	12	.34152	.00259
Educational professional	14	.34544	.00159

Variables	Order Selected	r^2	r^2 change
Value 4			
Political philosophy	1	.05647	.05647
Social work professional	5	.14034	.00781
Democrat			
Business professional	3	.11343	.02175
Independent politics			
Nontraditional religion	9	.16137	.00354
Psychology professional	7	.15339	.00536
Race/nonblack, white, Hispanic			
Political activity level			
Gender	2	.09168	.03521
Current family income	10	.16472	.00335
Character of current residence			
Nontraditional politics			
Divorced	12	.16932	.00207
Black			
Current residence in Northeast	13	.17122	.00190
Current residence in South			
Variables not selected by total value score			
White	6	.14803	.00769
Nursing professional	8	.15783	.00444
Republican	11	.16725	.00253
Roman Catholic	4	.13253	.01910
Protestant			
Jewish			
Character of birthplace			
Law professional			
Age			
Married			
Educational professional			
Current Residence in West	14	.17561	.00189

[a] Nonblacks, nonwhites, and non-Hispanics/Chicanos.

Political philosophy was the variable selected first in relation to total value score and for three out of four of the individual value scales. Membership in the profession of social work was selected first for one value scale and second for the total value score in addition to the remaining three value scales, a finding that supports its significance as identified in the three preceding chapters. Relationship to Democratic Party was selected third for two of the four individual value scales as well as for the total value score. Membership in business, psychology, and nursing most frequently were selected next. This identification of professions also validates previous findings. The order of the additional variables differed for each individual value scale as well as the total value score. Among those variables that were identified as contributing significantly to explaining score variance were political activity level and membership in the Republican Party. Religion did not enter the regression equation for total value score; it was entered fourth for value 4 and eleventh for value 1 when identification as a Roman Catholic was entered, followed by the twelfth variable, Protestant affiliation. The influence of current residence entered the equations for total score and two out of four of the individual scores relatively late. It was surprising that gender explained little of the variance for value 1, a fair amount for value 4, relatively little for the total value score, and an insignificant amount for values 2 and 3. Age was identified as contributing significantly only to the variance of value 3.

The first 10 variables selected by stepwise multiple regression for total value score explain 40 percent of the variance, leaving residual or unexplained variance of 60 percent. The next seven variables explain less than 1.5 percent additional variance. The fact that the second variable selected, membership in social work, is a dummy variable representing a type of profession introduces professional type as the second most important demographic variable in accounting for variance in the total value scores. The third variable selected, Democrat, also is a dummy variable introducing political party affiliation as the third most important variable contributing to the amount of variance explained. The fourth and fifth variables selected, membership in business and political registration as an independent, reinforce variables selected earlier in the regression model: professional type and political party affiliation. The sixth variable selected—nontraditional religion—also is a dummy variable that introduces religion as the next most important variable. The seventh variable—membership in the profession of psychology—adds additional support to the importance of professional type. The eighth variable selected—other races (nonblack, nonwhite, and non-Hispanic)—introduces the importance of race in explaining the variance in total value scores. This variable (race) also was set up as a series of dummy variables (presence versus absence). The ninth and tenth variables selected—political activity level and gender—identify both as explaining a significant amount of variance in total value scores.

The patterns of variables selected by the regressions for the four individual value scale scores differ to some extent from the pattern of variables selected in relation to total value scores. Table 15 illustrates, however, that many of the variables selected early in relation to total value score are similarly selected early by the model for each individual value scale. For example, in relation to value 1, the first five variables contain four out of five selected first by the model for total value scores. With respect to value 2, the first three variables reflect the same sequencing as that for the total value score. With respect to value 3, 10 out of the top 14 variables are similar to those selected by the regression for total value score. Not only were similar variables selected but the order of their selection was similar as well. For value 4, a similar pattern exists; nine of the first 17 variables were the same as those selected in relation to total value score.

For values 1 and 4, the variables selected as explaining a significant amount of variance of value scores collectively explain relatively small amounts of variance. For both value scales, the 14 variables selected by the regression models account for slightly more than 17.5 percent of variance. On the other hand, for value 2, 13 variables explain more than one-third of the total variance. For value 3, 14 variables explain more than 34.5 percent of the variance. For values 2 and 3, the variables selected explain an important amount of variance. The variables selected in relation to values 1 and 4, while explaining an important amount of variance, do so to a lesser degree.

Overall, these findings introduce a new dimension. Although professional type continues to be extremely important, political philosophy is even more important. Political philosophy and professional type, as introduced by affiliation with social work, explain the greatest amount of variance in individual value scale scores as well as total value scores. These variables are followed in importance by political party membership, current family income, and political activity level. Religion and gender played a less important role than anticipated, as did age, marital status, birthplace, geographic location of current residence, and characteristics of both locations. It was surprising, in light of previous findings, that number of years of professional experience also did not explain a significant amount of value score variance.

Members of different professions do differ in their overall value orientations. Those orientations, however, certainly are not determined solely by profession; rather, individuals with certain predispositions and particular life experiences seem to be more prone to selecting certain professions. And, in turn, professional education programs seem to accept those individuals with a greater propensity for adopting their overall value dimensions. The educational experience itself also plays an important role in value development. Although it is difficult to single out the impact of each individual demographic variable, it has been possible to identify their influence to an important, recognizable level.

Notes and References

1. See J. C. Kidneigh and H. W. Lundberg, "Are Social Work Students Different?" *Social Work,* 3 (July 1958), pp. 57–61; A. G. Cryns, "Social Work Education and Student Ideology: A Multivariate Study of Professional Socialization," *Journal of Education for Social Work,* 13 (Winter 1977), pp. 44–51; D. L. McLeod and H. J. Meyer, "A Study of the Values of Social Workers," in E. J. Thomas, ed., *Behavioral Science for Social Workers* (New York: Free Press, 1967), pp. 401–416; and A. Feld and R. Marks, "Self-Perceptions of Power: Do Social Work and Business Students Differ?" *Social Work,* 32 (May–June 1987), pp. 225–230.

2. D. B. James, *Poverty, Politics, and Change* (Englewood Cliffs, N.J.: Prentice-Hall, 1972).

3. J. W. Grimm and J. D. Orten, "Student Attitudes Toward the Poor," *Social Work,* 18 (January 1973), pp. 94–100.

4. McLeod and Meyer, "A Study of the Values of Social Workers."

5. Cryns, "Social Work Education and Student Ideology."

6. B. K. Varley, "Socialization in Social Work Education," *Social Work,* 8 (July 1963), pp. 102–109; B. K. Varley, "Are Social Workers Dedicated to Service?" *Social Work,* 11 (April 1966), pp. 84–91; and B. K. Varley, "Social Work Values: Changes in Value Commitments of Students from Admission to MSW Graduation," *Journal of Education for Social Work,* 14 (Fall 1968), pp. 67–76.

7. *For a description of multiple regression, including the stepwise option, see* chap. 35, "Regression," in *SPSS-X User's Guide* (2d ed.; Chicago: SPSS, 1986), pp. 662–686; M. J. Norusis, *SPSS-X Introductory Statistics Guide* (Chicago: SPSS, 1983), chap. 12, "Statistical Models for Salary: Multiple Linear Regression Analysis," pp. 135–174; and M. J. Norusis, *SPSS-X Advanced Statistics Guide* (Chicago: SPSS, 1985), chap. 2, "Modeling Salary: Multiple Linear Regression Analysis," pp. 9–71.

S·E·V·E·N

Marketplace:
A Comparison of Administrators and Direct Practitioners

♦

Preceding chapters have focused on a comparison of social workers with other professionals. Here the focus is directed toward a more detailed examination of social work professionals, and more specifically, a comparison of the differences between administrators and direct practitioners.

Throughout the years, both in schools of social work and in social service agencies, there has been undue competition between those social workers in administration and planning and those operating in direct services. This rift is evident among students, faculty, and practitioners alike and may be enhanced by differences in salary structure and power base.

Some research findings support these suggested differences; others reflect strong similarities. Recently, Feld and Marks substantiated the difference in their findings that the perceptions of power of social work students specializing in administration are more similar to those of business students than those of social workers in direct practice.[1] They also found gender to be significant in power perception differences. In her 1972 study of views of poverty, James found several factors contributing to professional differences: institutional/bureaucratic operations, use of the Freudian model, lack of training in dealing with public assistance, more concern with personal status than with social action, and movement up the professional prestige ladder, away from welfare positions.[2] Based on that, one could surmise that line workers or direct practitioners, by their very interaction with clients, might have a more positive attitude toward them than would administrators occupying positions higher in the bureaucratic structure. In examining social work attitudes toward the poor, Grimm and Orten also reported that the higher a worker is in the organization, the less likely he or she is to identify with clients (the poor).[3]

> *The growth of invisible complexity has called forth special professions to try to understand it; it has also called forth special professions to run it: administrators, managers, and a variety of technical specialists and applied scientists.*
> —R. N. Bellah et al., *Habits of the Heart*
> (New York: Harper & Row, 1985), p. 208.

In examining differences in commitment to the service ideal (the norms associated with delivery of service), Varley found major job responsibility to play a significant role.[4] Administrators indicated a stronger commitment to service ideals than did those social workers involved primarily in the direct delivery of services. This is contrary to the findings by James and Grimm and Orten. In examining differences in psychodynamic-mindedness, method of practice also was significant; direct practitioners scored higher than those involved in administrative capacities. In addition, Varley found political philosophy and gender to be significant in contributing to value score differences. In a later study, she also reported that social workers with a liberal political philosophy tended to score higher on most value scales than did northeasterners, administrators, younger people, and males.[5] Grimm and Orten also found age to be important.[6] Similar to Varley's results, their results revealed that the older the worker, the more negative his or her attitudes were toward the poor. People in an administrative capacity frequently are older; could age be responsible for value differences? Surprisingly, for Grimm and Orten, gender was not significant, but SES was. The lower the SES, the more negative were the attitudes toward the poor. If this is the case, administrators, with their upward mobility, should have more positive attitudes. On the whole, however, Grimm and Orten found direct practitioners (community organizers, 60 percent; caseworkers and group workers, 51 percent) to be more sympathetic than administrators (42 percent) toward the poor. They also reported nonsoutherners as having a more positive attitude toward the poor than southerners.

McLeod and Meyer found religion to play a major role in contributing to differences among social workers.[7] Kidneigh and Lundberg, on the other hand, found great homogeneity among social workers.[8] The social work groups examined by them reflected similar distributions on various demographic variables. Differences in experience and method of practice did not result in significantly different attitudes.

Based on an analysis of these research findings, together with the fact that all social workers should have experienced exposure to a similar value orientation, it was thought that no differences in POS value scores would exist between social workers in administration and those in direct practices, provided that the influence of age; gender; religion; political philosophy; political activity level; family income; region of residence; type of agency (public; private; nonprofit; and private, for-profit); and type of client served (based on SES) was controlled.

Sample

All social workers included in chapters 3 through 6, except for BSW students (chapter 3), were categorized on the basis of method of professional practice—direct service or administration. Beginning BSW students were not included because they typically are not expected to make such a career choice at entry to a generalist program. Most graduate students, on the other hand, select a method of practice at the time of application. Of the 699 usable subjects, 403 indicated direct service as the primary method of practice; 296 indicated administration as primary. Because no significant differences in value score means or variance of value scores existed among the three educational classifications (beginning students, recent graduates, and seasoned professionals), except for the differences between beginning students and social work faculty already noted, it was decided to include subjects from all three groups. Because of the identified differences between beginning social work students and social work faculty, faculty were included as a separate category rather than under the general heading of seasoned professionals. Data were analyzed separately for the three educational groups and the faculty category.

Comparision of Administrators and Direct Practitioners

No significant differences between the value scores of administrators and those of direct practitioners were noted in any of the categories except on value 3 for beginning students and recent graduates; these differences disappeared among seasoned professionals, including social work faculty (Table 16). In comparing the entire group of administrators with the direct practitioners, no significant differences in value scores were noted. The differences in Table 16 are supported by further statistical tests. A summary of F scores and probability levels are presented in Table A-24, appendix A.

A comparison of administrators and direct practitioners from the group of beginning students (graduate level) indicated that the two groups were homogeneous with respect to age, gender, race, sexual preference, marital status, number of children, current living arrangements, political party affiliation, political philosophy, political activity level, birthplace, characteristics

Table 16.
POS Value Score Means for Direct Practitioners and
Social Work Administrators

Method of Practice	n	Value 1	Value 2	Value 3	Value 4
Beginning students	140	42.89	37.96	31.05	43.46
Direct practice	106	42.86	37.93	31.82*	43.42
Administration	34	42.97	38.06	28.65*	43.56
Recent graduates	81	44.01	39.30	33.25	43.70
Direct practice	63	44.35	39.73	33.94*	43.65
Administration	18	42.83	37.78	30.83*	43.89
Seasoned professionals	336	43.52	38.20	33.30	43.78
Direct practice	140	43.76	38.14	33.21	44.23
Administration	196	43.34	38.24	33.37	43.46
Social work faculty	142	43.76	39.27	34.06	43.46
Direct practice	94	43.94	39.28	34.24	43.69
Administration	48	43.42	39.25	33.71	43.02
Total	699	43.50	38.50	33.00	43.64
Direct practice	403	43.66	38.60	33.20	43.80
Administration	296	43.28	38.36	32.73	43.43

* = $p < .05$

of birthplace, current residence, characteristics of current residence, current family income, parents' educational levels, amount of previous work experience, and financial auspices of place of employment. Chi-squares between the two groups with respect to the preceding variables revealed no significant differences between groups. Religion was the only demographic variable for which significant differences were found ($\chi^2 = 15.02$; $df = 4$; $p < .005$).[9] Proportionally, there were twice as many Protestants in the administrative category, twice as many Jews in direct practice, and four times as many people expressing no religious affiliation in direct practice. The preceding supports earlier findings by McLeod and Meyer that Protestants scored lower on social work value dimensions; Jews and those with no religious affiliation scored higher.[10] Although students came to social work with an apparent predisposition to its professional value base, they completed POS before having any exposure to social work courses. It is logical that earlier convictions, such as those influenced primarily by religious beliefs, would remain paramount, only to be refined later through the educational and professional socialization process.

Examination of demographic differences between administrators and direct practitioners in the other three groups of social workers revealed that recent graduates differed significantly with respect to political party affiliation ($\chi^2 = 16.14$; $df = 3$; $p < .001$). Proportionally, 10 times as many administrators as direct practitioners proclaimed themselves Republicans.

One-third fewer administrators identified themselves as Democrats; twice as many direct practitioners identified themselves as independents. Seasoned professionals differed with respect to age ($\chi^2 = 18.64$; $df = 4$; $p < .001$) and birthplace ($\chi^2 = 12.28$; $df = 4$; $p < .015$). Direct practitioners tended to be younger than administrators. Proportionally, half again as many administrators were born in the Northeast; twice as many direct practitioners were born in the Midwest. One could speculate that the old adage about northeasterners being more competitive and aggressive and midwesterners being more laid back and beneficent may be grounded in solid reality. Northeasterners may be more prone to assuming administrative responsibilities; midwesterners, direct practice positions. In comparing administrators and direct practitioners among social work faculty, significant differences were noted with respect to age ($\chi^2 = 8.15$; $df = 3$; $p < .05$), gender ($\chi^2 = 14.23$; $df = 1$; $p < .001$), and characteristics of current residence ($\chi^2 = 9.50$; $df = 4$; $p < .05$). Faculty in direct practice were both significantly younger and older than those in administration, who tended as a group to hover around middle age. Proportionally, there were twice as many males in administration as in direct practice faculty positions. Three times as many male administrators lived in major metropolitan areas, and twice as many direct practitioners lived in suburban areas.

Taken collectively, the administrators and direct practitioners also were significantly different with respect to income and years of experience. As might be expected, administrators had significantly more experience and, in turn, had significantly higher incomes. The data here show that 6 percent of direct practitioners earn less than $15,000 and 41 percent earn more than $45,000. Four percent of administrators earn less than $15,000 and 47 percent, more than $45,000.

There were no significant differences in variance of value scores between administrators and direct practitioners with the exception of beginning students on value 3. Controlling for the influence of several variables was justified because the two groups did differ demographically. Analyses of covariance did not render additional significant differences in variance of value scores between the two methods of practice (Table A-25, appendix A). Political philosophy emerged as the most significant covariate in three out of four groups of social workers (beginning students, seasoned professionals, and social work faculty/field instructors); this was followed in importance by political activity level among beginning social work students, political party affiliation among recent graduates, and religion and age among seasoned professionals. Controlling for covariates still failed to result in significant differences in value scores between the two social work methods groups with the exception of value 3 for beginning students and value 1 for recent graduates.

Although administrators and direct practitioners claim to be different breeds, they both appear to reflect the same underlying social work values;

that is, they are operating under the influence of the same overarching principles. Suspected differences may be based on different styles rather than different underlying values. By their very responsibilities, administrators may present a more directive, controlling stance; they may have been selected in the first place because of their underlying organizational and managerial abilities. Direct practitioners, with primary responsibilities on a one-on-one or small-group interactional level, may seem more reserved. Because of underlying personality dynamics, they most likely opted for this level of intervention. It may be a clash between styles of intervention, coupled with personality attributes, that creates the feeling of apparent conflict between social workers in administration and those in direct practice when, in reality, a philosophical clash is nonexistent.

It is reassuring that members of two major segments of the social work profession (administrators, who are primarily responsible for directing the focus of social service agencies, and direct practitioners, who are responsible for delivering services to clients) appear to be united around a common value base. Every social worker, no doubt, can recall blatant conflict between administrators and direct practitioners. Unfortunately, such conflict may interfere with collaboration, development, and implementation of solid plans for service delivery. It could be speculated that in a hierarchical situation, there often is conflict similar to that between parent and child, or the underling versus the authority figure. The underlying values of both may be quite similar, however. It is hoped that, for the most part, such transference–countertransference issues, such apparent conflicts, are addressed fully by social work professionals. It is probably safe to assume, however, that some vestiges of conflict remain, although evidence to that effect is minimal.

One also could speculate about why conflicts between the two methodological foci appear early in the educational process. It may be the initial phenomenon of jockeying for position or hierarchical delineation. The bottom line, however, is that social work is a united profession with a common value base for all its members—whether their primary method is administration or direct practice. These findings substantiate the idea of professional socialization around a solid professional philosophy and underlying value base.

Notes and References

1. A. Feld and R. Marks, "Self-Perceptions of Power: Do Social Work and Business Students Differ?" *Social Work,* 32 (May–June 1987), pp. 225–230.

2. D. B. James, *Poverty, Politics, and Change* (Englewood Cliffs, N.J.: Prentice-Hall, 1972).

3. J. W. Grimm and J. D. Orten, "Student Attitudes Toward the Poor,"

Social Work, 18 (January 1973), pp. 94–100.

4. B. K. Varley, "Are Social Workers Dedicated to Service?" *Social Work,* 11 (April 1966), pp. 94–91.

5. B. K. Varley, "Social Work Values: Changes in Value Commitments of Students from Admission to MSW Graduation,"*Journal of Education for Social Work,* 14 (Fall 1968), pp. 67–76.

6. Grimm and Orten, "Student Attitudes Toward the Poor."

7. D. L. McLeod and H. J. Meyer, "A Study of the Values of Social Workers," in E. J. Thomas, ed., *Behavioral Science for Social Workers,* (New York: Free Press, 1967), pp. 401–416.

8. J. C. Kidneigh and H. W. Lundberg, "Are Social Work Students Different?" *Social Work,* 3 (July 1958), pp. 57–61.

9. Yates' correction for small frequencies within cells was used when necessary. *See SPSS-X User's Guide* (2d ed.; Chicago: SPSS, 1986), p. 346.

10. McLeod and Meyer, "A Study of the Values of Social Workers."

EIGHT

Socialization, Life Experience, and Value Orientation:
Their Influence on Social Work Practice

The eighties is a time identified by current writers, such as Allan Bloom, Robert B. Reich, and Robert Bellah and his colleagues, as one marked by increased conservatism and heightened individualism.[1] It thus is encouraging that social workers continue to set a tone reflecting respect for basic rights, social responsibility, individual freedom, and self-determination that far exceeds that of their peers in other major professions. At each career level (beginning student, recent graduate, and seasoned professional) and in both major methods of professional practice (direct practice and administration), social workers surpass members of other professional groups in their commitment to the four basic values espoused as being important by the profession. Although values are influenced by the tenor of the times—including the current period of increased conservatism and individualism—social workers continue to respond in a fashion reflecting the same sociopolitical biases historically attributed to them. While other professions appear to have been influenced dramatically by the times, social work has continued to enforce its stance as a protector of social rights and a promoter of social justice.

It is safe to say that social workers are different. These findings run counter to alarming earlier data collected by James, which suggested that social work values had become obfuscated by upward mobility, with its attention to individualism and ethnocentrism.[2] In light of the current resurgence of individualism identified by Bellah and his colleagues, it is indeed remarkable that social workers have managed to recapture and sustain their traditional value stance.[3] It is not surprising, however, considering their major mission as "conscience setters" of society.[4]

Emphasis within the profession of social work itself certainly has highlighted the importance of the four values measured by POS. The CSWE accreditation standards have consistently emphasized both values and respect for cultural diversity (with an increased emphasis on respect for cultural diversity in more recent standards) as two critical criteria for program accreditation.[5] The NASW *Code of Ethics*, together with such recent developments as the Committee on Inquiry—a vehicle for adjudication related to infractions of the *Code of Ethics*—have emphasized social responsibility, respect for clients' rights, and—foremost—ethical behavior grounded on the professional value structure. The focus of social work curricula, with

---

The recent education of openness . . . pays no attention to natural rights or the historical origins of our regime, which are now thought to have been essentially flawed and regressive. It is progressive and forward-looking. It does not demand fundamental agreement or the abandonment of old or new beliefs in favor of the natural ones. It is open to all kinds of [people], all kinds of life-styles, all ideologies. There is no enemy other than the [person] who is not open to everything. But when there are no shared goals or vision of the public good, is the social contract any longer possible?
—A. Bloom, *The Closing of the American Mind,* p. 27.

---

their emphases on ethical imperatives and appreciation of diversity, has facilitated the development of moral decision making and, in turn, a socially responsible mindset. An emphasis on respect for diversity is accompanied by an appreciation for the other and a valuing of actions that incorporates consideration of the common good. All contribute to a heightened sense of social responsibility marked by movement away from narcissism and toward increased respect and consideration for all of society.

Differences at Various Career Points

Comparisons of social workers at various career points, no matter where they are in their careers, reveal that their values exceed those of their peers in other professions. Beginning social work students come to the profession harboring the results of "anticipatory socialization," Hayes and Varley's term for the self-socialization that occurs in prospective students before they are admitted to social work education.[6] Beginning students also are screened carefully by admissions committees that are well aware of the standards stressed in the profession. Recent graduates, having been exposed to curricular content espoused by accreditation standards, exhibited even greater concurrence with social work values than did beginning students. They showed greater value concurrence than did their peers from other professional degree programs. Seasoned professionals also exhibited a stronger commitment to social work values than any of their equally seasoned peers in other professions. Their concurrence with the four basic social work values was less than that of recent social work graduates but more than that of beginning students. This may be a reflection of the typical learning curve that results in some loss of material immediately after initial mastery, or it may result from the influence of educational programs that place less emphasis on values, cultural diversity, and moral decision making. Or it may depend on the fact that seasoned professionals and beginning students and recent graduates, are products of different eras.

Although providers of the two primary methods of social work practice (direct practice and administration) are noted for their proclaimed differences, no significant differences were found between the two groups with respect to values. The converse appeared to be the case, supporting a united identity for the profession. Practitioners of both major methods of practice presented evidence of similar value orientations. Despite major differences in their delivery of service, administrators and direct practitioners seemed guided by the same set of underlying principles in their actions.

Overall Influence of Demographics

At all points along the career ladder, certain demographic factors emerged as critical. Prior research indicated that at the beginning of one's career, religion,[7] gender,[8] age,[9] birthplace,[10] SES,[11] rural–urban dimensions of residence, and political philosophy[12] are important.

Demographic variables played a significant role in determining the value perspective of undergraduate students. When the influence of the foregoing variables was controlled, significant differences in value scores among the various undergraduate professions disappeared except for value 3. At the graduate level, differences did not disappear when the influence of the specified demographics was controlled. It may well be that the graduate students, because of their increased maturity and additional educational experience, are influenced less emphatically by their more distant past. Undergraduate students, on the other hand, by their inexperience and greater immaturity, obviously are still influenced greatly by earlier demographic effects and are less able, and perhaps less prepared, to assert themselves or to move in another direction.

The demographic variable that explained the greatest amount of variance for undergraduates was religion, followed by family income, birthplace, age, and current region of residence. There is a high correlation between birthplace and current region of residence for undergraduates ($r = .872$); thus, both are measures of the same phenomenon. (For graduates, the correlation between the two was much lower: $r = .267$.) All the preceding variables support the contention that early home–family experiences are important for undergraduate students in determining their value orientation and professional choice. For beginning graduate students, who had left the nest some time ago and had already had at least four years of college experience, external factors (or those outside the family) seemed to play a more significant role. Political philosophy emerged as the most important demographic variable in relation to all four value scores. Although other more basic variables (birthplace, current region of residence, gender, rural–urban dimensions of residence, age, and religion) explained significant levels of variance, they were insufficient in eliminating significant differences among the value scores of the professions being examined. Despite the significance of the various demographics, important differences remained among the value scores of the various groups.

Recent graduates continued to present similar patterns; strong differences in value orientation continued to exist between social work and the other professions. Earlier research noted a reduction in value scores between beginning students and recent graduates.[13] This reduction actually reflected a change in values to approximate more closely those of seasoned professionals. Students entering a program had higher values than those of seasoned professionals. During the students' involvement in the educational program, their values were modified to reflect those of the seasoned professionals. Values of recent graduates in this study reflected an increase over values of beginning students, rather than a decrease, and the movement was also in the direction of that espoused by the seasoned professional group.

Demographics by Importance

Throughout initial analyses of the groups of professionals at the three points in time, professional type was the major dimension being examined. In all cases, it was assigned a position of priority in the analyses, and, in all cases, it proved significant at all points in the career ladder, with social workers scoring higher on all value scales. In explanations of the influence of the profession in relation to all other demographic variables, professional type retained a high priority; it was surpassed in importance, however, by political philosophy (conservative, moderate, and liberal). This could be

Table 17.
Summary of Correlations between Political Philosophy
and Professional Type

Profession	r
Social work	.148
Psychology	.078
Law	.021
Medicine	−.002
Education	−.056
Nursing	−.087
Business	−.182

interpreted as the underlying philosophy being more important than profession. It is critical to note that political philosophy and profession are not mutually exclusive. Rather, an examination of correlations between the various professions and political philosophy reveals a relationship (Table 17).

The values in Table 17 were obtained by correlating political philosophy, which was scored from 1, conservative, to 5, liberal, and membership in a particular profession, which was coded 1 for membership and 0 for nonmembership. The values presented indicate that a greater percentage of social workers are more liberal, followed by professionals in psychology, law, medicine, education, nursing, and business. An examination of correlations between profession and political philosophy reveals that, for social workers, professional membership is positively related to increased liberalness. For business, membership in that profession is negatively related to increased liberalness; this could be translated to mean that membership in that profession is positively related to increased conservatism.

It seems that social work has risen to Michael Austin's challenge,[14] that the discipline has forgotten the squabble about professional status and has begun to spend its time defining its overall mission. Although it may not have been spelled out to the extent desired, social work as an entirety expresses values that reflect its underlying value base, and that value base sets the tone for specific attitudes toward current social issues. Based on the content of POS, social workers scored significantly higher on the four identified values. Those scores were derived from liberal attitudes toward the content of the 41 Public Social Policy Statements espoused by NASW, the primary source for content of POS.

Additional Observations

The data speak clearly for themselves; some methodological limitations should be mentioned, however. There are distinct limitations to the sample pool. First of all, the sample pool is only reflective of three universities, all in the Northeast. Although the sample size in general is adequate, it should be larger in relation to specific subsamples—for example, medicine—especially at the level of seasoned professionals.

The data are not longitudinal; rather, they were collected from three separate groups reflecting three distinct periods. Such collection allows for comparison of three time periods but does not allow for examination of overall individual value change over time.

Initially, it was determined that the four value scales in POS would reflect a hierarchy, with most people scoring higher on value 1 and with greater discrepancies arising between professionals as one moves down the value hierarchy. In other words, more subjects would concur with value 1 and fewer subjects would concur with value 4 with gradations in between. This was not the case, possibly owing to the process of selection of the items to be included in the scale. The process included removing those items on which it was thought everyone would agree. This removal may have had an important bearing on the hierarchical outcome of value scores, or rather the lack of proposed hierarchy structure. The items were removed before the original factor analysis, so the result of their possible inclusion remains to be determined.

On the whole, however, POS—designed specifically to measure concurrence with the four primary values reflecting the underlying value base of the profession—appears to be a suitable instrument for identifying and measuring differences in values. In this case, POS was able to identify differences in value orientation among the seven major professions being examined.

A word of caution must be offered about the use of dummy variables. First, their use requires more degrees of freedom, resulting in less sensitive tests. Second, their influence cannot be considered a slope but rather is more representative of the magnitude of an effect (presence versus absence) or a constant contributor.

Correlations support the multitude of interdependencies among the variables. Although efforts were made to develop a statistical design for data analyses that would isolate the influence of the variables to the greatest extent possible, variables (under the current limitations of survey and value research) never can be isolated completely.

On the whole, after the influence of the demographic variables was controlled, differences in values among the professionals continued to exist, with social workers topping others on the four values measured by POS. Yes, social workers as a group are different. Social workers tend to start out that way and to continue that way throughout their careers. They tend to refine and maintain those differences in light of their basic underlying professional philosophy. It appears that CSWE-accredited curricula facilitate professional socialization in the desired direction, although additional examination would be necessary to obtain stronger verification. It also appears that professional socialization for social work is an important dynamic process that begins before entry into the profession and continues strongly throughout membership. Increased identification with underlying social work values is included in the process. The process creates professionals—social workers—who remain distinct from members of other professions despite the strong pull toward value modification by the larger society.

Implications for Practice

What are the implications for practice? How do social workers apply these values they possess? Do these values make social workers more effective?

The implications for practice are crucial. Trained social workers as a group present commitment to the values highlighted here that goes well beyond the commitment or focus of their peers in other professions. As a group, social workers enter the professional arena with a heightened awareness of clients' rights and their own personal responsibility to protect and facilitate the exercising of those rights. This means not only making individual professional judgments or taking individual professional action; it also includes activity along a larger perspective, one involving advocacy and political action. As a group, social workers have actively supported political candidates who endorse values espoused by their profession; they also have publicized the policies and political candidates who have not.

The development of the National Center for Social Policy and Practice is an indication of the profession's commitment to using research findings and policy analyses to promote change in the direction of greater compliance with the values of the profession. The political action arm of NASW, Political Action for Candidate Election, has served a vital role in supporting political candidates who espouse platforms compatible with professional social work values.

If opinions, in fact, do reflect underlying values—and values do influence behavior—social workers are by their very orientation more aware of their social responsibility to promote the well-being of others and are more active in fulfilling that responsibility. As a professional group, social workers also place greater credence on the importance of individual freedom and of encouraging individual choice (self-determination). The literature reflects the profession's commitment to a particular set of values; the list of NASW's professional sanctions against individuals and agencies presents additional evidence of the importance it places on adhering to those values. Classroom content that focuses not only on basic values but also on the necessary ingredients for implementing those values, such as respect for diversity, women's issues, minority concerns, the "isms," and opposition to institutional oppression, helps instill this basic value orientation. Each year the topic of NASW Social Work Month expands the awareness of both the profession and the public about critical societal injustices—injustices identified on the basis of the underlying value scheme.

This certainly is not to say that other professions are unconcerned about societal issues surrounding people's well-being. Many members of other disciplines are committed deeply to such a stance. As a group, however, professionally trained social workers are different; their very profession is built on this clearly defined value base. Indeed, at the foundation of social work is a base that attracts certain individuals to the profession, a theme that is highlighted throughout the educational experience, and a pervasive force that is well integrated in the underlying professional belief system and that sets the parameters for the behavioral repertoire exhibited by professional social workers in their everyday lives.

Notes and References

1. A. Bloom, *The Closing of the American Mind* (New York: Simon & Schuster, 1987); R. B. Reich, *Tales of a New America* (New York: Times Books, 1987); and R. N. Bellah et al., *Habits of the Heart* (New York: Harper & Row, 1985).

2. D. B. James, *Poverty, Politics, and Change* (Englewood Cliffs, N.J.: Prentice-Hall, 1972).

3. Bellah et al., *Habits of the Heart.*

4. J. L. Vigilante, "Between Values and Science: Education for the Profession During a Moral Crisis or Is Proof Truth?" *Journal of Education for Social Work,* 10 (Fall 1974), pp. 107–115.

5. *For standards in operation since 1984, see* CSWE Commission on Accreditation, *Handbook of Accreditation Standards and Procedures* (New York: Council on Social Work Education, 1984); *for earlier standards, see* CSWE Commission on Accreditation, *Manual of Accrediting Standards for Graduate Professional Schools of Social Work* (New York: Council on Social Work Education, 1971); and CSWE Commission on Accreditation, *Standards for Accreditation of Baccalaureate Degree Programs in Social Work* (New York: Council on Social Work Education, 1974).

6. D. D. Hayes and B. K. Varley, "Impact of Social Work Education on Students' Values," *Social Work,* 10 (July 1965), pp. 40–46.

7. D. L. McLeod and H. J. Meyer, "Chapter 30: A Study of the Values of Social Workers," in E. J. Thomas, ed., *Behavioral Science for Social Workers* (New York: Free Press, 1967).

8. Hayes and Varley, "Impact of Social Work Education on Students' Values"; and J. C. Kidneigh and H. W. Lundberg, "Are Social Work Students Different?" *Social Work,* 3 (July 1958), pp. 57–61.

9. McLeod and Meyer, "Chapter 30."

10. Hayes and Varley, "Impact of Social Work Education on Students' Values."

11. J. W. Grimm and J. D. Orten, "Student Attitudes Toward the Poor," *Social Work*, 18 (January 1973), pp. 94-100; and B. K. Varley, "Socialization in Social Work Education," *Social Work*, 8 (July 1963), pp. 102-109.

12. Varley, "Socialization in Social Work Education."

13. B. K. Varley, "Social Work Values: Changes in Value Commitments of Students from Admission to MSW Graduation," *Journal of Education for Social Work*, 14 (Fall 1968), pp. 67-76.

14. M. Austin, "The Flexner Myth and History of Social Work," *Social Service Review*, 57 (September 1983), pp. 357-377.

A·P·P·E·N·D·I·X A

Professional Opinion Scale:
An Instrument for Determining Value Orientation

◆

Influence of Earlier Social Work Value Scales

The development of POS (appendix B) was strongly influenced by suggestions generated by earlier social work attitude scales.[1] From a methodological perspective, the human attitude scale developed by Howard and Flaitz is the most influential one to date.[2] They initially selected 150 items representing six dimensions—(1) social justice, (2) social action/social responsibility, (3) human nature, (4) human rights, (5) civil rights, and (6) individual autonomy and freedom—in relation to a broad range of social issues. Using factor analysis, they identified those items with the highest degree of relatedness along some common dimension. The scale used a 5-point, Likert-type format with approximately one-half the items worded negatively; it was validated on the basis of content and face validity. Items that loaded on more than one factor were eliminated. Those 10 items with the strongest loading on the appropriate scale were retained. A minimum loading of 0.20 was necessary for inclusion.

Based on the foregoing, five factors were retained that accounted for approximately 33 percent of the trace or variance. Using varimax rotation and the previously mentioned criteria, only four factors were ultimately retained: (1) social justice, (2) individual freedom, (3) human nature, and (4) human rights. Cronbach alpha reliability coefficients yielded scores indicating strong internal consistency within each subscale. A second administration of the scale (the shortened 40-item version) produced subscales supporting those identified in the initial testing.

The researchers identified several methodological concerns. The sample size of the initial group ($n = 110$) was too small, and the two samples used should have been more similar. (Their first sample consisted of undergraduate and graduate students in programs other than social work, but the second consisted exclusively of social work graduate students.) They believed that the four remaining subscales should have been rerotated after dropping the fifth subscale, and nonorthogonal or oblique rotation rather than varimax rotation should have been used based on the relatedness of the scales and items. An additional limitation involved the fact that their scale was designed solely to measure extent of identification "with humanistic positions toward selected 'socioprofessional' concerns,"[3] all items being developed by the researchers themselves. Thus, the scope is limited and may not measure the broader spectrum of values espoused by the social work profession.

Rationale for POS

POS was developed in light of the paucity of instruments designed to identify and measure degree of concurrence with the underlying ideology or value base of social work, as well as the current resurgence of interest in professional social work values. Development of POS was based on the assumption that the value base of any profession should be evident in the public social policy or position papers of the major professional organization involved—in this case, NASW. A second assumption was that one's opinions reflect one's underlying value base.[4] Because of their breadth and timeliness, it seemed most appropriate that the NASW Public Social Policy Statements be used as the source of statements composing POS. In addition, because NASW members developed the statements, it was believed that the influence of the underlying value base should be evident in the statements themselves.

Development of the NASW Public Social Policy Statements

The NASW Public Social Policy Statements are developed by members and endorsed by the Delegate Assembly, the national legislative body of NASW, which meets triennially (biennially until 1981) to review and establish policy for guiding its Board of Directors.[5] Three hundred delegates (approximately one per 250 members) are elected to represent their colleagues, who are divided into 55 chapters, including all 50 states, metropolitan New York, the District of Columbia, Puerto Rico, the Virgin

Islands, and Europe. The number of delegates is based on chapter membership; each chapter has at least one delegate and one alternate. Approximately 10 to 14 percent of the membership votes in these elections, which are conducted in compliance with affirmative action standards of the association. National NASW reports an election ballot return rate of 14 to 16 percent, with 12 to 14 percent in Pennsylvania, 12 percent in New Jersey, 13 percent in Maryland, 9 to 10 percent in Missouri, and 8 to 10 percent in metropolitan Washington, D.C.

During the three-day triennial meeting, delegates are expected to develop operational policies and procedures to guide the association and to formulate resolutions determining desired courses of action for the association. They are also expected to determine priorities for the next three-year period and to endorse policy statements that reflect NASW's principles or plans with respect to professional issues, social policy issues, and organizational policies.

The policy statements are formulated by NASW members, chapters, or various membership groupings. A specific format for submission includes information on who is presenting the policy, the policy category (social, professional, or organizational), the issue to be addressed, a summary of major components of the policy, background data, and the actual detailed policy statement.[6]

Policy statements must be submitted to the national office of NASW approximately one year before a Delegate Assembly. This allows sufficient time for an editorial review of the statements by the Executive Committee; the effect of such a policy on existing policies and/or other proposed policies can be determined and the statements redrafted if necessary. Any revisions must be completed in time to assure delivery to delegates at least three months before an assembly. Policies that do not receive board approval may be submitted for delegate action with the board's opinion appended. Proposed policies that have not been examined and circulated in advance may be brought before the assembly by a petition signed by at least 500 NASW members from at least five chapters. Additional policies, introduced while the assembly is in session, must go through the usual review procedures and must be brought before a subsequent assembly for deliberation. Based on the preceding, it is clear that the development of policy statements is indeed a thorough and serious matter.

Development of POS Items from the Public Social Policy Statements

In developing POS, the principal investigator developed 200 statements designed to reflect the content of the entire set of NASW Public Social Policy Statements. These items were examined for clarity and accuracy by two graduate social work research assistants. The 200-item version of POS was administered to eight additional social workers—four with DSWs, four with MSWs, all with at least 10 years of direct practice experience, and all with some social work teaching experience. Those items that were considered ambiguous by these eight respondents were eliminated. Based on the preceding criteria, 121 items were retained in the final version of POS, a 5-point Likert-type scale. Items were assigned positions using a table of random numbers; approximately one-half the items were worded negatively to avoid respondent bias.

Format of POS

Directions for completion of POS were printed on the cover of the scale booklet. Respondents were asked to select one of the answers that most accurately reflected their opinion of the statement: (A) strongly agree, (B) agree, (C) neutral, (D) disagree, and (E) strongly disagree. Respondents were asked to record their answers on a computer-scoreable answer sheet using a number 2 pencil. The 121-scale items were followed by 26 items designed to collect demographic information, such as age, gender, race, marital status, political party affiliation, religious affiliation, political philosophy, geographic area of origin (birthplace), present area of residence,[7] and socioeconomic status.[8] Respondents also were asked to record their social security number or any other number unique to them to facilitate data organization.

Pilot Testing of POS

Initially, POS was given to a pilot pool of 600. The respondents who replied by the end of the first month of data collection were assigned to sample 1 ($n = 203$); the remaining respondents, who replied by the end of the next month ($n = 310$), were alternately distributed to sample 2 ($n = 155$) and sample 3 ($n = 150$; five were unusable). Eighty-seven from the original pilot group did not respond. Approximately one-third of the pilot group came from social service agencies located in New Jersey, Pennsylvania, and Delaware. Copies of the scale were mailed to agencies following telephone agreement to participate. The agencies were selected to reflect diversity: public agencies, private agencies, health care facilities; some provided services to children and their families, welfare recipients, the handicapped, middle- and upper-class individuals; a range of religions were represented. An additional third was recruited by sending two copies of POS to a wide range of individuals with instructions asking that they complete one copy of the scale and give the second copy to a colleague who could be considered quite different philosophically from themselves. These individuals resided primarily in New Jersey, Pennsylvania, New York, and Delaware. The remaining third of the group was recruited from summer school classes. The goal of the method of data collection—to assure a sample of wide variability among recipients—was achieved.

Appendix A

Table A-1 illustrates some basic characteristics of the samples generated from the pilot group. Respondents included both BSW and MSW students and graduates, social work faculty and field instructors, social service agency staff members, and students in business.

A review of Table A-1 illustrates that the three samples generated from the pilot group were comparable except for sample 2. Sample 2 had less than one-half the proportion of agency staff and almost twice as many social work graduates, faculty, and field instructors as either sample 1 or sample 3. This was not of major concern because the categories social work graduates and social work faculty and field instructors represent the field of social work, and many of these individuals were most likely affiliated with social service agencies. Table A-2 presents an overview of demographic characteristics of the three samples that reinforces their comparability.

Initial Identification of POS Value Subscales: Sample 1

The responses of sample 1 to the entire 121 items within POS were examined by means of principal components factor analysis.[9] Criteria used for factoring were a minimum eigen value of 1, a minimum factor loading of 0.4, the elimination of those items that loaded on more than one factor, and a maximum number of 25 rotation iterations. This initial factor analysis, which used varimax rotation, resulted in six factors (dimensions), which explained 28 percent of the trace or variance. A decision was made to drop the sixth factor because it contained only three items with significant loadings. Because of the limited number of items in each and their related content, the fourth and fifth factors were combined into one dimension. The 10 items in each factor with the highest loadings were retained. Table A-3 contains a listing of items composing each factor. Based on the values identified in the literature and the content of the factor items, the four factors (values) have been labeled: (1) respect for basic rights, (2) sense of social responsibility, (3) commitment to individual freedom, and (4) support of self-determination.

The values, as identified, appear to support a hierarchy emphasizing the moral decision making espoused by social work, with each successive value more strongly reflective of the underlying social work value base. For moral decision making to occur, an individual must be able to overcome narcissism while simultaneously increasing commitment to the greater whole or the common good. Thus, each successive value represents greater movement away from self and toward respect for and appreciation of the other.

A second analysis of sample 1 was conducted using nonorthogonal or oblique rotation with only the 40 items making up the four factors. A four-factor limit was imposed, as well as a minimum factor loading of 0.3 and a maximum of 50 rotation iterations. Sample 1 converged in 21 iterations, with the four subscales explaining 36.6 percent of the variance. A comparison of factor loadings, with those loadings generated using the 121 items, reinforces selection of the four subscales (Table A-4). Although producing Cronbach alpha reliability coefficients slightly below those using all 121 items,[10] the coefficients based on 10 items per factor indicate acceptable levels of internal consistency for each dimension (Table A-5).

Second Analysis of POS: Sample 2

To determine accuracy and reliability of the dimensions identified in the original factor analysis, the 40 items comprising the four dimensions were analyzed in sample 2 using nonorthogonal rotation. They were subjected to the same criteria as were those in sample 1: a four-factor limit, minimum factor loading of 0.3, and a maximum of 50 rotation iterations. Sample 2 converged in 19 iterations, with the four factors explaining 34.5 percent of the variance. A comparison of factor loadings (Table A-4) and alpha reliability coefficients (Table A-5) strongly reinforces the factors identified in sample 1. All items except for three loaded significantly on the appropriate subscale. Items 16 and 35 in factor 3 loaded more heavily on factor 1, and item 24 in factor 4 loaded more heavily on factor 2. Item 96 in factor 2 fell short of the 0.3 minimum factor loading.

This replication was encouraging. It constituted a crossvalidation of the factors identified in sample 1.

Third Analysis of POS: Sample 3

The purpose of dividing the pilot group into three samples was to afford two opportunities for replicating. The 40 items constituting the four factors in sample 3 were analyzed using the same procedures and criteria as were employed with sample 1 and sample 2. Sample 3 converged in 41 iterations, with the four factors explaining 36.7 percent of the variance. A comparison of factor loadings (Table A-4) and alpha reliability coefficients (Table A-5) strongly supports the factors (dimensions) identified in sample 1. With the exception of five items in factor 4, all items loaded on the appropriate factor. Items 19, 24, 33, 105 loaded more heavily on factor 1; item 101 loaded more heavily on factor 2. This second replication again speaks to the construct validity of the identified factors.

Face Validity of POS

In addition to the aforementioned replications, three judges (one MSW practitioner, one PhD practitioner/educator, and one DSW educator) were asked to sort the 121 items composing POS into the four identified value dimensions. This process yielded 80 percent or more interjudge agreement. Comparing their sortings with the factors generated in sample 1 yielded agreement of 69 percent of more, thus providing additional support for the four value dimensions.

Sensitivity of POS to Variability

Besides concern about the reliability and validity of POS, an additional concern existed over its ability to pick up differences in degree of concurrence with the various value dimensions. To determine its effectiveness in this capacity, the three pilot samples were combined and divided into five main respondent categories: (1) social work students, (2) social work graduates, (3) social work faculty, (4) social service agency personnel, and (5) business students. An examination of the value score means illustrates that POS can differentiate among groups on the basis of type of professional socialization (Table A-6). Social work students, recent graduates, faculty and field instructors, and social service agency personnel scored higher on all four value scales than did business students, a category made up of about one-half graduate students and one-half undergraduates.

Box-plots graphically illustrate the value score differences among the various respondent categories (Figure A-1). The box-plots[11] indicate the median score for each value by respondent category together with the 50 percent spread (25 percent to 75 percent) around each value median.

Results of analyses of variance[12] support the fact that respondent types do differ significantly on scores received on the four identified value subscales (Table A-7); however, as illustrated by the comparison of value means (Table A-6) and the box-plots (Figure A-1), this relationship appears to result primarily from the presence of the business students. When the business students were removed from the data set, analyses of variance on the value scores of the four social work-related respondent types yielded no significant differences on three out of four values. The only significant difference was on value 3.

Scores were obtained by using Tukey's Honestly Significant Difference and Scheffe's test,[13] both of which were designed to override the inherent bias in multiple comparisons of means. Results support noted differences between business students and the remaining four categories (all of which reflect various degrees of professional social work socialization) (Table A-8). It was somewhat disturbing that, except for social work students/social work graduates versus social work faculty on value 3, no significant differences were noted among the four value scores of the various social work respondent categories. This finding is surprising considering their purported differences in degree of professional socialization. This may have been a result of the small sample size and the similarities of sample subjects—the majority of the sample subjects were from the greater mid-Atlantic megalopolis, with all students, faculty, and field instructors representing the same major state university.

Figure A-1.
Box-Plots for Value Scores by Respondent Type

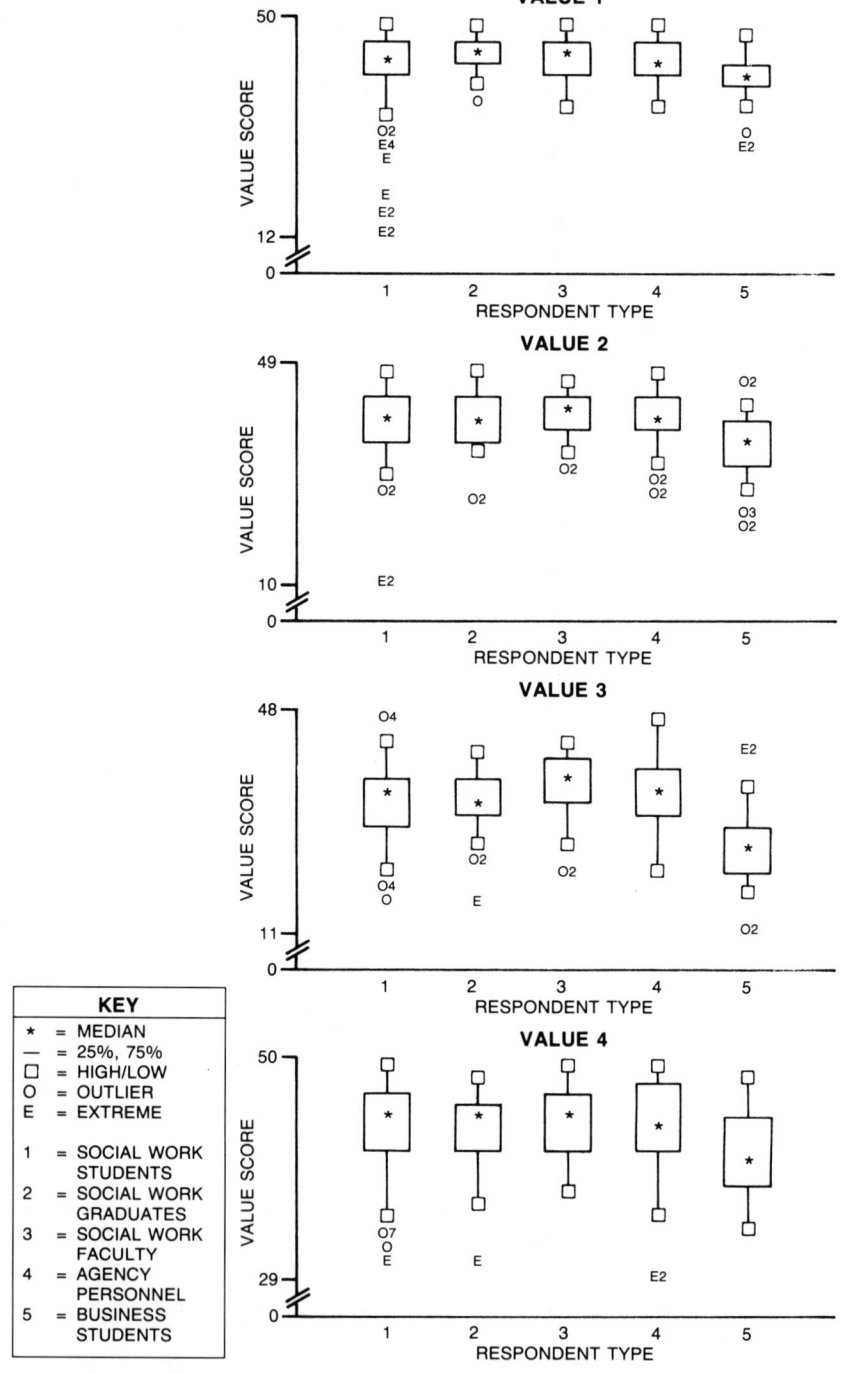

Appendix A

Influence of Demographics

When the influence of various background variables was removed (Table A-9), the noted differences between the business and social work categories remained. The differences on value 3 noted when only the four social work categories were compared disappeared, suggesting the important contribution of the demographic variables. In analyses involving all respondent types and *only* the four social work types, the one significant covariate with respect to all four values was underlying political philosophy. When examining *only* social work respondent types, political activity level was significant with respect to values 1, 2, and 3. Religion was significant with respect to value 1; political party membership and family income, with respect to value 2; and age, with respect to value 4.

In analyses involving both business and social work respondent categories, the significant covariates were political philosophy on all four values, political activity level on three values, age and family income on two values, and political party membership on one value.

Additional Support for Initial Factors

The responses of the three largest respondent categories—(1) social work students, (2) social service agency personnel, and (3) business students—were analyzed by means of principal components factor analysis with the same criteria as were used with the three pilot samples. Table A-10 illustrates the generation of value factors by these three respondent categories. Composition of the value categories (factors) remained consistent; however, the factor ordering varied among groups. The factor composition illustrates the strength of the factors; the factor ordering demonstrates the ability of POS to differentiate among groups.

Cronbach alpha reliability coefficients for the value factors generated by the three respondent categories (type 1, social work students; type 4, social service agency personnel; and type 5, business students) (Table A-11) also provide additional support for the composition of the four values.

Scoring POS

The factor weightings were used to determine factors. For scoring purposes, the weightings were not used; rather, answers were given a score from 1 to 5. This was determined by comparing scores using the factor weightings from sample 1 (the largest sample) and those based on factor loadings from sample 2 and sample 3, respectively (Table A-12). Because of the similarity of scores based on sample 1 and sample 2 loadings and on sample 1 and sample 3 loadings, along with small sample sizes, it was decided that loadings of 1 for each item were most appropriate.

Summary

The preceding tests indicate that POS has sufficient levels of reliability and validity to warrant its use in the collection of data reflecting degree of concurrence with the four identified social work values. It also has sufficient ability to recognize individual differences and to differentiate on the basis of such differences.

POS represents a beginning step in the identification and measurement of professional social work values. Although still considered exploratory (and in its early developmental stages), POS provides sufficient evidence of reliability and validity. Additionally, POS appears to be sensitive to individual differences, although further examination should be conducted to compare its assessment with that of other measures of value orientation. Additional applications should include more diverse populations and experimental or educational conditions.

The development of POS reinforces the use of principal components analysis as an appropriate method of identifying factors. The second analysis of sample 1 using only the 40 items comprising the four factors reinforces those factors identified in the original application. Use of the two additional samples—sample 2 and sample 3—offers additional support for the accuracy and stability of the factors. Although the generation of dimensions using factor analysis is based on procedures without regard for content or meaning, the value dimensions found in POS do appear to contain related items. There is considerable evidence that the four factors (dimensions) are valid and that they do reflect basic underlying values of the social work profession.

POS appears to examine values advocated by the social work profession. It also provides a valid and practical means for assessing degree of concurrence with these basic identified values.

Notes and References

1. See B. K. Varley, "Socialization in Social Work Education," *Social Work*, 8 (July 1963), pp. 102-109; D. L. McLeod and H. J. Meyer, "Chapter 30: A Study of the Values of Social Workers," in E. J. Thomas, ed., *Behavioral Science for Social Workers,"* (New York: Free Press, 1967), pp. 401-416; and T. U. Howard and J. Flaitz, "A Scale to Measure the Humanistic Attitudes of Social Work Students," *Social Work Research and Abstracts*, 18, No. 4 (Winter 1982), pp. 11-18.

2. Howard and Flaitz, "A Scale to Measure the Humanistic Attitudes of Social Work Students."

3. Ibid., p. 12.

4. J. Meddin, "Attitudes, Values and Related Concepts: A System of Classification," *Social Science Quarterly*, 55 (1975), pp. 889-900.

5. *For an overview of the composition of NASW Delegate Assembly, see The Delegate Assembly Handbook—1984 Delegate Assembly* (Silver Spring, Md.: National Association of Social Workers, 1984).

6. *For detailed guidelines for policy development, see* "Appendix B: Guidelines for Preparation of Policy Statements for the 1984 Delegate Assembly," in *Delegate Assembly Manual* (Silver Spring, Md.: National Association of Social Workers, 1984).

7. The following was used as a guide in determining geographic regions: J. Garreau, *The Nine Nations of North America* (Boston: Houghton Mifflin, 1981).

8. Questions about parents' educational level (one of the key indicators used by Hollingshead in his "Index of Social Position," as reported in A. B. Hollingshead and F. C. Redlich, *Social Class and Mental Illness* [New York: John Wiley & Sons, 1958]) were used to determine socioeconomic status.

9. *For an overview of factor analysis, see* J. Kim and C. W. Mueller, *Introduction fo Factor Analysis: What It Is and How to Do It* (Beverly Hills, Calif.: Sage Publications, 1978; J. Kim and C. W. Mueller, *Factor Analysis: Statistical Methods and Practical Issues* (Beverly Hills, Calif.: Sage Publications, 1978); chapter 37, "Factor," in *SPSS-X User's Guide* (2d ed., Chicago: SPSS Inc., 1986).

10. *SPSS-X User's Guide (2d ed.; Chicago: SPSS Inc., 1986), pp. 857–859.*

11. *For information on developing box-plots, see* chapter 28, "Manova: General Linear Models," in *SPSS-X* (2d ed.; Chicago: SPSS Inc., 1986), pp. 505–506.

12. *For an overview of variance and covariance, see* J. H. Bray and S. E. Maxwell, *Multivariate Analysis of Variance* (Beverly Hills, Calif.: Sage Publications, 1985); G. R. Iverson and H. Norpoth, *Analysis of Variance* (Beverly Hills, Calif.: Sage Publications, 1976); *and* A. R. Wildt and O. T. Ahtola, *Analysis of Covariance* (Beverly Hills, Calif.: Sage Publications, 1978).

13. *For an overview of multiple comparison of means, see* A. J. Klockars and G. Sax, *Multiple Comparisons* (Beverly Hills, Calif.: Sage Publications, 1986).

Table A-1.
General Characteristics of the Three Pilot Samples

	Sample 1		Sample 2		Sample 3	
Sample Characteristic	n	%	n	%	n	%
BASW student	4	1.97	3	1.94	4	2.67
MSW student	86	42.36	64	41.29	53	35.33
BASW/MSW graduate	12	5.91	19	12.26	12	8.00
Faculty/field instructor	10	4.93	19	12.26	10	6.67
Agency staff	68	33.50	25	16.13	50	33.33
Business student	23	11.33	25	16.13	21	14.00
Total	203	100.00	155	100.01	150	100.00

Table A-2.
Specific Characteristics of the Pilot Samples

	Sample 1 ($n = 203$)		Sample 2 ($n = 155$)		Sample 3 ($n = 150$)	
Characteristic						
Age						
Under 25	36	17.7	31	20.1	32	21.3
26–35	69	34.0	50	32.3	50	33.3
36–45	58	28.6	46	29.7	40	26.7
46–55	30	14.8	18	11.6	20	13.3
Over 55	9	4.4	10	6.5	7	4.7
Missing	1	0.9	0	0	1	0.7
Gender						
Male	52	25.6	40	25.8	36	24.0
Female	149	73.4	113	72.9	112	74.7
Missing	2	0.9	2	1.3	2	1.3
Race						
Black	20	9.9	22	14.2	13	8.7
Caucasian	166	81.8	126	81.3	123	82.0
Hispanic	8	3.9	6	3.9	6	4.0
Other	7	3.4	1	0.6	6	4.0
Missing	2	0.9	0	0	2	1.3
Marital status						
Single	70	34.5	50	32.3	61	40.7
Married	93	45.8	72	46.5	63	42.0
Divorced	29	14.3	25	16.1	18	12.0
Widowed	2	1.0	3	1.9	1	0.7
Other	8	3.9	5	3.3	6	4.0
Missing	1	0.5	0	0	1	0.7
Number of children						
0	106	52.2	79	51.0	83	55.3
1	28	13.8	21	13.5	19	12.7

Table A-2. (Continued)

Characteristic	Sample 1 (n = 203)		Sample 2 (n = 155)		Sample 3 (n = 150)	
2–3	49	24.1	41	26.5	34	22.7
4–5	15	7.4	12	7.7	11	7.3
More than 5	4	2.0	2	1.3	2	1.3
Missing	1	0.5	0	0	1	0.7
Political party						
Republican	31	15.3	21	13.5	24	16.0
Democratic	108	53.2	84	54.2	77	51.3
Independent	32	15.8	27	17.4	21	14.0
Other	3	1.5	1	0.6	3	2.0
None	27	13.3	22	14.2	23	15.3
Missing	2	0.9	0	0	2	1.3
Political philosophy						
Liberal	67	33.0	55	35.5	49	32.7
Moderate	104	51.2	74	47.7	76	50.7
Conservative	17	8.4	16	10.3	13	8.7
Other	12	5.9	8	5.2	9	6.0
Missing	3	1.8	2	1.3	3	2.0
Religion						
Jewish	34	16.7	20	12.9	26	17.3
Protestant	61	30.0	42	27.1	42	28.0
Roman Catholic	63	31.0	57	36.8	46	30.7
Other	16	7.9	15	9.7	4	7.3
None	24	11.8	19	12.3	20	13.3
Missing	5	2.7	2	1.3	5	3.3
Family income						
Less than $15,000	19	9.4	10	6.5	16	10.7
$15,000–19,999	29	14.3	14	9.0	22	14.7
$20,000–29,999	60	29.6	42	27.1	39	26.0
$30,000–44,999	48	23.6	44	28.4	31	20.7
More than $45,000	39	19.2	42	27.1	34	22.7
Missing	8	3.9	3	1.9	8	5.3
Highest degree						
High school	9	4.4	12	7.7	9	6.0
Associate's	3	1.5	3	1.9	2	1.3
Bachelor's	106	52.5	76	49.0	71	47.3
Master's	65	32.0	43	27.7	51	34.0
Post-master's	10	4.9	13	8.4	8	5.3
Missing	10	4.9	8	5.2	9	6.0
Years of experience						
0–5	94	46.3	69	44.5	70	46.7
6–10	30	14.8	37	23.9	21	14.0
11–15	30	14.8	16	10.3	22	14.7

Table A-2. (Continued)

Characteristic	Sample 1 (n = 203)		Sample 2 (n = 155)		Sample 3 (n = 150)	
16–20	20	9.9	13	8.4	14	9.3
More than 20	13	6.4	6	3.9	9	6.0
Missing	16	7.9	14	9.0	14	9.3

Table A-3.
Items Comprising the Four POS Value Dimensions

Factor 1: Respect for Basic Rights

Item Number	Content
27.	Retirement at 65 should be mandatory.
37.	Abduction by parents who do not have custody should be viewed as a family, not a legal, matter.
39.	The government should not subsidize family planning programs.
43.	The mandatory retirement age protects society from the incompetence of the elderly.
55.	Mandatory retirement based on age should be eliminated.
65.	The aged require only minimum mental health services.
74.	Only medical personnel should be involved in life and death treatment decisions.
75.	Pregnant adolescents should be excluded from school.
79.	Students should be denied government funds if they participate in protest demonstrations.
83.	Juveniles do not need to be provided with legal counsel in juvenile courts.

Factor 2: Sense of Social Responsibility

	Content
20.	There should be a guaranteed minimum income for everyone.
25.	The federal government has invested too much money in the poor.
26.	The government should not redistribute the wealth.
52.	The government should provide a comprehensive system of insurance protection against loss of income because of disability.
62.	Local governments should be monitored on their enforcement of civil rights statutes.
89.	Unemployment benefits should be extended, especially in areas hit by economic disaster.
92.	The gap between poverty and affluence should be reduced through measures directed at redistribution of income.

Table A-3. (Continued)

96.	The government has primary responsibility for helping the community accept a returning offender.
97.	Efforts should be made to increase voting among minorities.
100.	"No-knock" entry, which allows the police entrance without search warrant, encourages police to violate the rights of individuals.

Factor 3: Commitment to Individual Freedom
Content

2.	All direct-income benefits to welfare recipients should be given in the form of cash.
16.	The employed should have more government assistance than the unemployed.
18.	Sterilization is an acceptable method of reducing the welfare load.
35.	The FBI should keep files on individuals with minority political affiliation.
46.	Welfare mothers should be discouraged from having more children.
51.	Capital punishment should not be abolished.
61.	The death penalty is an important means for discouraging criminal activity.
66.	Welfare workers should keep files on those clients suspected of fraud.
85.	Corporal punishment is an important means of discipline for aggressive, acting-out adolescents.
90.	It would be better to give welfare recipients vouchers or goods rather than cash.

Factor 4: Support of Self-Determination
Content

13.	When they are old enough, children should have the right to choose their religion, including the option to choose none.
19.	Counseling should be available to women who ask for abortions.
24.	Couples should decide for themselves whether they want to become parents.
31.	Women should have the right to use abortion services.
33.	The dying have a right to be informed of their prognosis.
50.	Family planning should be available to all adolescents.
101.	Family planning services should be available to individuals regardless of income.
105.	Older persons should be sustained to the extent possible in their own environments.
110.	The child in adoption proceedings should be the primary client.
113.	A family may be defined as two or more individuals who consider themselves a family and who assume protective, caring obligations to one another.

Table A-4.
Comparison of Factor Loadings on Value Dimension Items

Value	Sample 1 (121 items) n = 203	Sample 1 (40 items) n = 203	Sample 2 (40 items) n = 155	Sample 3 (40 items) n = 150
Factor 1: Respect for Basic Rights				
27	0.522	0.637	0.370	0.613
37	0.451	0.586	0.541	0.491
39	0.443	0.487	0.344	0.467
43	0.571	0.715	0.546	0.595
55	0.416	0.523	0.334	0.579
65	0.494	0.446	0.522	0.520
74	0.427	0.544	0.654	0.492
75	0.430	0.425	0.449	0.305
79	0.456	0.642	0.682	0.501
83	0.497	0.444	0.538	0.322
Factor 2: Sense of Social Responsibility				
20	0.435	0.545	0.499	0.501
25	0.506	0.618	0.541	0.558
26	0.443	0.637	0.691	0.560
52	0.437	0.565	0.487	0.570
62	0.504	0.575	0.386	0.587
89	0.536	0.623	0.455	0.480
92	0.523	0.637	0.635	0.602
96	0.478	0.353	0.299	0.403
97	0.497	0.628	0.455	0.653
100	0.481	0.475	0.355	0.435
Factor 3: Commitment to Individual Freedom				
2	0.410	0.540	0.628	0.375
16	0.417	0.339	a	0.419
18	0.486	0.501	0.410	0.577
35	0.436	0.346	a	0.475
46	0.513	0.591	0.626	0.564
51	0.587	0.711	0.587	0.727
61	0.658	0.691	0.661	0.701
66	0.503	0.558	0.638	0.570
85	0.469	0.437	0.528	0.427
90	0.582	0.680	0.681	0.596
Factor 4: Support of Self-Determination[b]				
13[c]	0.454	0.366	0.340	0.354
19[d]	0.441	0.521	0.460	a
24[d]	0.432	0.354	e	a
31[c]	0.519	0.584	0.644	0.536
33[d]	0.632	0.555	0.488	a
50[c]	0.434	0.562	0.579	0.644

Table A-4. (Continued)

	Sample 1 (121 items) n = 203	Sample 1 (40 items) n = 203	Sample 2 (40 items) n = 155	Sample 3 (40 items) n = 150
101[d]	0.530	0.624	0.586	e
105[d]	0.531	0.533	0.507	a
110[d]	0.409	0.391	0.420	a
113[c]	0.494	0.477	0.421	0.426

[a]Loads more heavily on factor 1.
[b]Factor 4 and factor 5 were combined into factor 4.
[c]Item contained in initial factor 5.
[d]Item contained in initial factor 4.
[e]Loads more heavily on factor 2.

Table A-5.
POS Value Subscale Reliability Coefficients

Value	Original Factoring (121 items)	POS Subscales[a] (40 items)		
	Sample 1 (n = 203)	Sample 1 (n = 203)	Sample 2 (n = 155)	Sample 3 (n = 150)
Factor 1	0.795	0.7879	0.7317	0.7782
Factor 2	0.802	0.7773	0.7269	0.7756
Factor 3	0.817	0.7934	0.7914	0.7984
Factor 4	0.717	0.7027	0.6733	0.6575

Cronbach alpha reliability coefficients are used.
[a]Items with loadings below 0.4 were dropped; the top 10 items in each factor (value) were retained.

Table A-6.
Comparison of Value Scores for Various Respondent Types

Type	n	Value 1		Value 2		Value 3		Value 4	
		Mean	SD	Mean	SD	Mean	SD	Mean	SD
1	212	42.32	6.16	38.28	5.37	33.09	6.26	43.34	4.42
2	43	44.12	3.48	37.95	5.12	32.44	5.37	43.67	3.75
3	39	43.64	3.76	39.13	4.56	35.90	6.03	43.80	3.39
4	141	43.39	3.79	38.53	4.71	34.62	5.41	43.67	4.22
5	50	40.30	4.74	33.64	6.38	25.56	6.91	40.90	4.57
Missing	27								
Total	508	42.69		37.91		32.89		43.25	

1 = social work students; 2 = social work graduates; 3 = social work faculty; 4 = social service agency personnel; 5 = business students.

Table A-7.
Summary of ANOVAs on Value Scores by All Respondent Types

Value	F	p
1	3.160	.0100
2	4.186	.0010
3	19.511	.0000
4	4.687	.0010

Results of Analyses of Variance (ANOVAs) on Value Scores by Social Work Respondent Types

Value	F	p
1	2.464	.0620
2	.456	.7160
3	4.339	.0050
4	.267	.8492

Table A-8.
Significant Differences between Respondent Types Based on Tukey's Honestly Significant Difference

Value	Type 1 1　2　3　4	Type 2 1　2　3　4	Type 3 1　2　3　4	Type 4 1　2　3　4	Type 5 1　2　3　4
Type 2					
Value 1	NS				
Value 2	NS				
Value 3	NS				
Value 4	NS				
Type 3					
Value 1	NS	NS			
Value 2	NS	NS			
Value 3	.05	.05			
Value 4	NS	NS			
Type 4					
Value 1	NS	NS	NS		
Value 2	NS	NS	NS		
Value 3	NS	NS	NS		
Value 4	NS	NS	NS		
Type 5					
Value 1	.05	.05	.05	.05	
Value 2	.05	.05	.05	.05	
Value 3	.05	.05	.05	.05	
Value 4	.05	.05	.05	.05	

NS = not significant.

Table A-9.
Results of Analysis of Covariance of Respondent Type on Value Scores, Controlling for the Influence of Various Demographic Variables

All Five Respondent Types		
Value	F	p<
1	3.374	.010
2	7.702	.000
3	16.454	.000
4	4.576	.001

Significant Covariates in Descending Order of Importance for all Five Respondent Types		
Value	F	p
Value 1		
Political philosophy	43.990	.000
Political activity level	20.187	.000
Family income	5.250	.022
Value 2		
Political philosophy	42.672	.000
Political activity level	18.965	.000
Family income	11.098	.001
Political party membership	8.320	.004
Age	5.074	.025
Value 3		
Age	53.881	.000
Political philosophy	31.905	.000
Political activity level	7.162	.008
Value 4		
Political philosophy	37.274	.000

Four Social Work Respondent Types		
Value	F	p<
1	2.326	.074
2	.368	.776
3	1.918	.126
4	.797	.496

Significant Covariates in Descending Order of Importance for Four Social Work Respondent Types		
Value	F	p
Value 1		
Political philosophy	40.837	.000
Political activity level	13.514	.000
Religion	5.060	.025
Value 2		
Political philosophy	33.660	.000

Table A-9. (Continued)

Political activity level	14.379	.000
Political party membership	9.394	.002
Family income	7.832	.005
Value 3		
Age	23.235	.000
Political philosophy	22.175	.000
Political activity level	8.771	.003
Value 4		
Political philosophy	25.202	.000
Age	4.808	.029

Table A-10.
Factor Loadings on Value Scale Items for Various Respondent Types

Value	Sample 1 (n = 203)	Type 1[a] (n = 212)	Type 4[b] (n = 141)	Type 5[c] (n = 50)
Factor 1: Respect for Basic Rights				
27	0.637	0.489	0.542	0.437
37	0.586	0.572	0.442	0.436
39	0.487	0.642	[d]	0.475
43	0.715	0.719	0.484	0.411
55	0.523	0.427	0.606	0.608
65	0.446	0.460	0.482	0.545
74	0.544	0.753	0.415	0.401
75	0.425	0.572	[e]	0.689
79	0.642	0.721	0.518	[e]
83	0.444	0.703	0.432	[d]
Factor 2: Sense of Social Responsibility				
20	0.545	0.497	0.514	−0.671
25	0.618	[f]	0.656	−0.633
26	0.637	0.366	0.741	−0.452
52	0.565	[d]	0.491	−0.706
62	0.575	[f]	[d]	−0.409
89	0.623	0.449	0.513	−0.645
92	0.637	0.493	0.638	−0.623
96	0.353	<.300	[d]	[e]
97	0.628	[f]	[f]	−0.546
100	0.475	[e]	[e]	−0.448
Factor 3: Commitment to Individual Freedom				
2	0.540	0.419	[f]	0.643
16	0.339	[f]	[f]	0.413
18	0.501	0.569	[g]	0.788
35	0.346	[f]	[f]	0.468

Table A-10. (Continued)

Value	Sample 1 (n = 203)	Type 1[a] (n = 212)	Type 4[b] (n = 141)	Type 5[c] (n = 50)
46	0.591	0.652	0.361	0.769
51	0.711	0.689	0.699	0.617
61	0.691	0.676	0.557	0.480
66	0.558	0.611	d	0.348
85	0.437	0.439	0.680	0.705
90	0.680	0.393	f	0.603
Factor 4: Support of Self-Determination				
13	0.366	0.501	0.541	g
19	0.521	e	0.373	f
24	0.354	0.463	f	f
31	0.584	0.539	0.674	0.350
33	0.555	e	e	−0.429
50	0.562	0.703	0.612	f
101	0.624	0.496	0.493	f
105	0.533	e	0.542	0.313
110	0.391	e	e	f
113	0.477	0.422	0.343	−0.539

[a]Order of factors generated: 1, 3, 2, 4.
[b]Order of factors generated: 1, 2, 3, 4.
[c]Order of factors generated: 3, 1, 2, 4.
[d]Loads more heavily on factor 4.
[e]Loads more heavily on factor 3.
[f]Loads more heavily on factor 1.
[g]Loads more heavily on factor 2.

Table A-11.
POS Subscale Reliability Coefficients for Various Respondent Types

	POS Subscales[a] (40 items)			
Factor	Sample 1 (n = 203)	Type 1 (n = 212)	Type 4 (n = 141)	Type 5 (n = 50)
1	0.7879	0.8400	0.6322	0.6373
2	0.7773	0.7328	0.7103	0.8176
3	0.7934	0.7696	0.7081	0.8103
4	0.7027	0.6705	0.7453	0.6582

Cronbach alpha reliability coefficients are used.

[a]Items with loadings below 0.4 were dropped; the top 10 items in each factor were retained. In factor 1, one item was dropped; factor 2, two items; factor 3, three items; and factors 4 and 5, which were combined as factor 4, five items.

Table A-12.
Comparison of Value Means Based on Sample Factor Loadings
for the Three Pilot Samples

	Sample 1	Sample 2		Sample 3	
Value	One loadings	Two loadings	One loadings	Three loadings	One loadings
1	23.21	21.19	22.99	20.89	23.38
2	21.66	18.15	21.51	20.22	21.43
3	17.24	18.53	16.77	17.60	17.06
4	21.66	20.75	21.46	19.98	21.56

Table A-13.
Summary of ANOVAs in Value Scores of Beginning Students
by Profession and Educational Level

Value	F	$p <$
Undergraduate		
Value 1	2.930	.023
Value 2	2.790	.029
Value 3	8.584	.000
Value 4	3.267	.014
Graduate		
Value 1	4.800	.000
Value 2	15.284	.000
Value 3	12.525	.000
Value 4	4.747	.000

Table A-14.
Summary of Chi-Square Values for Demographic Variables and
Professional Type at the Beginning Student Level

Variable	χ^2	df
Undergraduate level		
Age	46.97***	12
Gender	21.61***	4
Political party	27.19**	12
Religion	32.12**	16
Father's educational level	31.91**	16
Mother's educational level	28.10*	16
Graduate level		
Age	58.84***	20

Table A-14. (Continued)

Variable	χ^2	df
Gender	92.10***	20
Political party	59.59***	20
Political philosophy	47.39***	20
Political activity	58.42***	20
Family income	42.24**	20
Father's educational level	41.34**	20
Mother's educational level	38.27**	20

* = $p < .05$; ** = $p < .01$; *** = $p < .001$.

Table A-15.
Results of Analyses of Covariance of Beginning Student Respondent Type on Value Scores, Controlling for the Influence of Various Demographic Variables

Beginning Undergraduate Students		
Value	F	$p<$
1	1.337	.260
2	2.354	.057
3	7.411	.000
4	2.081	.087

Significant Covariates in Descending Order of Importance for Beginning Undergraduate Students		
Value	F	p
Value 1		
Family income	5.417	.022
Region of birth	5.368	.022
Current region of residence	4.119	.044
Value 2		
Religion	4.206	.042
Value 3		
Age	4.961	.028
Value 4		
Religion	5.598	.019
Family income	4.393	.038

Beginning Graduate Students		
Value	F	$p<$
1	3.621	.003

Table A-15. (Continued)

Beginning Graduate Students		
Value	F	p<
2	11.397	.000
3	10.055	.000
4	3.401	.005

Significant Covariates in Descending Order of Importance for Beginning Graduate Students		
Value	F	p
Value 1		
Political philosophy	35.019	.000
Region of birth	21.162	.000
Current region of residence	16.107	.000
Gender	10.674	.001
Rural/urban region of residence	8.207	.004
Religion	3.892	.049
Value 2		
Political philosophy	38.419	.000
Age	8.520	.004
Gender	6.449	.011
Religion	5.482	.020
Value 3		
Political philosophy	25.443	.000
Age	12.649	.000
Region of birth	10.765	.001
Religion	9.630	.002
Gender	4.877	.028
Value 4		
Political philosophy	21.738	.000
Gender	18.241	.000
Rural/urban region of residence	12.156	.001
Religion	5.353	.021

Table A-16.
Summary of ANOVAs in POS Value Score Means
by Profession and Educational Level for 1986 Graduates

Value	F	p<
Undergraduate		
Value 1	7.822	.000
Value 2	13.965	.000
Value 3	15.130	.000
Value 4	5.104	.002

Table A-16. (Continued)

Value	F	p<
Graduate		
Value 1	6.716	.000
Value 2	11.761	.000
Value 3	12.430	.000
Value 4	3.518	.009

Table A-17.
Summary of Chi-Square Values for Demographic Variables and Profession for Recent Graduates

Variable	χ^2	df
Undergraduate graduates		
Gender	11.07*	3
Political party	36.35***	12
Political philosophy	19.06*	9
Father's educational level	23.35*	12
Graduate graduates		
Age	48.86***	16
Gender	11.01*	4
Political party	50.99***	16
Political philosophy	45.65***	12
Family income	52.92***	16
Father's educational level	29.24*	16

* = $p < .05$; *** = $p < .001$.

Table A-18.
Summary of Analyses of Covariance of Graduate Professional Type on Value Scores, Controlling for the Influence of Various Demographic Variables

Undergraduate Graduates		
Value	F	p<
1	4.871	.003
2	8.447	.000
3	11.128	.000
4	3.968	.009

Table A-18. (Continued)

Significant Covariates in Descending Order of Importance for Undergraduate Graduates		
Value	F	p
Value 1		
Current residence	17.341	.000
Political philosophy	11.904	.001
Gender	11.396	.001
Value 2		
Family income	21.858	.000
Political philosophy	10.630	.001
Value 3		
Race	10.511	.001
Family income	10.450	.001
Political philosophy	5.000	.027
Value 4		
Gender	12.808	.000

Graduate Graduates		
Value	F	$p <$
1	4.983	.001
2	6.694	.000
3	10.946	.000
4	3.656	.007

Significant Covariates in Descending Order of Importance for Graduate Graduates		
Value	F	p
Value 1		
Political philosophy	10.314	.002
Value 2		
Political philosophy	11.178	.001
Family income	10.733	.001
Race	7.768	.006
Religion	6.673	.011
Value 3		
Gender	4.695	.032
Political philosophy	4.212	.042
Race	3.982	.048
Value 4		
Gender	4.383	.038

Table A-19.
Summary of Chi-Square Values Examining Demographic Variables by Professional Type

Variable	χ^2	df	p
Age	74.41	24	.001
Gender	102.01	6	.001
Race	9.01	18	NS
Sexual preference	1.72	12	NS
Marital status	12.67	24	NS
Number of children	22.64	24	NS
Political party	70.04	24	.001
Political philosophy	66.27	18	.001
Religion	46.99	24	.001
Region of birth	67.51	24	.001
Current residence	67.39	24	.001
Character of residence	52.80	24	.001
Current income	89.45	24	.001
Father's educational level	18.77	24	NS
Mother's educational level	14.80	24	NS

NS = not significant.

Table A-20.
Summary of ANOVAs in Value Scores of Seasoned Professionals

Value	F	p<
1	18.630	.000
2	29.398	.000
3	31.455	.000
4	18.019	.000

Table A-21.
Results of Analyses of Covariance of Seasoned Professionals on Value Scores, Controlling for the Influence of Various Demographic Variables

Value	F	p<
1	13.925	.000
2	18.769	.000
3	22.438	.000
4	14.394	.000

Table A-21. (Continued)

Value	F	p
Significant Covariates in Descending Order of Importance		
Value 1		
Political philosophy	43.176	.000
Gender	10.301	.001
Major work setting[a]	5.054	.025
Value 2		
Political philosophy	92.255	.000
Current family income	15.884	.000
Religion	12.164	.001
Type of clients[b]	8.028	.005
Major work setting	8.024	.005
Value 3		
Political philosophy	74.096	.000
Current family income	21.358	.000
Religion	15.083	.000
Age	14.643	.000
Political activity	7.756	.005
Type of clients	5.112	.024
Number of years in profession	5.063	.025
Value 4		
Political philosophy	39.935	.000
Age	6.714	.010
Religion	6.380	.012
Gender	6.177	.013
Number of years in profession	5.873	.016

[a]Public versus privately funded setting.
[b]Income/professional level of clients.

Table A-22.
Results of Two-Way ANOVAs by Profession and Point in Professional Career (Time)

	F	p<
Professions based on undergraduate degrees		
Value 1		
Professional type	42.659	.000
Time	18.845	.000
Profession by time	1.026	.406
Value 2		
Professional type	72.244	.000
Time	4.107	.017

Table A-22. (Continued)

	F	p<
Profession by time	2.380	.027
Value 3		
Professional type	89.402	.000
Time	25.090	.000
Profession by time	.571	.754
Value 4		
Professional type	38.983	.000
Time	7.752	.000
Profession by time	1.419	.204
Professions based on graduate degrees		
Value 1		
Professional type	30.928	.000
Time	6.371	.002
Profession by time	2.239	.023
Value 2		
Professional type	64.260	.000
Time	3.581	.028
Profession by time	1.205	.292
Value 3		
Professional type	62.632	.000
Time	16.863	.000
Profession by time	2.277	.020
Value 4		
Professional type	28.839	.000
Time	1.173	.310
Profession by time	1.803	.072

Table A-23.
Correlation Coefficients between Key Demographic Variables

Variables	r
Age × single marital status	−.517
Age × married marital status	.375
Age × number of children	.593
Age × family income	.280
Age × father's educational level	−.288
Age × mother's educational level	−.257
Single marital status × number of children	−.624
Married marital status × number of children	.544
Divorced marital status × family income	−.184
Married marital status × family income	.441
Mother's educational level × father's level	.609

Table A-23. (Continued)

Variables	r
Birthplace (Northeast) × current residence (Northeast)	.333
Birthplace (South) × current residence (South)	.238
Birthplace (Midwest) × current residence (Midwest)	.353
Birthplace (West) × current residence (West)	.314
Republican × political philosophy	−.323
Republican × political activity level	.041
Democrat × political philosophy	.186
Democrat × political activity level	.210
Family income × political philosophy	−.040
Family income × political activity level	.140

Table A-24.
Summary of ANOVAs of Value Scores for Social Work Administrators and Direct Practitioners

Level of Practitioner	Value 1	Value 2	Value 3	Value 4
Beginning student	.017	.018	6.890**	.033
Recent graduate	2.321	1.997	3.453	.043
Seasoned professional	.934	.026	.043	2.990
Faculty/field instructor	.593	.001	.240	.864
Total group	1.534	.335	.904	1.505

** = $p < .01$.

Table A-25.
Results of Analyses of Covariance of Social Work Administrators and Direct Practitioners on Value Scores, Controlling for the Influence of Various Demographic Variables

Beginning students		
Value	F	p<
1	.006	.939
2	.021	.974
3	8.452	.004
4	.001	.979
Significant Covariates in Descending Order of Importance for Beginning Students		
Value	F	p
Value 1		
Political philosophy	16.242	.000
Political activity level	3.954	.049

Table A-25. (Continued)

Value	F	p
Value 2		
Political philosophy	14.796	.000
Religion	4.848	.029
Political activity level	4.654	.033
Value 3		
Political philosophy	9.064	.003
Religion	5.694	.018
Value 4		
None		

Recent graduates

Value	F	$p <$
1	1.059	.037
2	.713	.401
3	.115	.735
4	1.618	.208

Significant Covariates in Descending Order of Importance for Recent Graduates

Value	F	p
Value 1		
None		
Value 2		
Current family income	7.918	.006
Gender	5.826	.018
Political party affiliation	4.259	.043
Value 3		
Political party affiliation	6.679	.012
Value 4		
Political party affiliation	5.660	.020

Seasoned professionals

Value	F	$p <$
1	.995	.319
2	.412	.521
3	.221	.638
4	1.189	.276

Significant Covariates in Descending Order of Importance for Seasoned Professionals

Value	F	p
Value 1		
None		
Value 2		
Political philosophy	16.518	.000
Religion	7.656	.006

Table A-25. (Continued)

Value	F	p
Value 3		
Political philosophy	19.039	.000
Religion	7.390	.007
Age	7.104	.008
Value 4		
Political philosophy	12.047	.001
Age	8.813	.003

Faculty/Field Instructors		
Value	F	p<
1	.275	.601
2	.208	.649
3	.224	.637
4	.017	.897

Significant Covariates in Descending Order of Importance for Faculty/Field Instructors		
Value	F	p
Value 1		
None		
Value 2		
Political philosophy	3.967	.048
Value 3		
None		
Value 4		
Political philosophy	7.301	.008
Gender	4.543	.035

APPENDIX B

Professional Opinion Scale

June 1985

◆

Directions: PLEASE USE A NO. 2 LEAD PENCIL TO MARK YOUR ANSWERS.

Answer all items on the enclosed NCS Answer Sheet using a no. 2 pencil.
A on the answer sheet = Strongly Agree
B on the answer sheet = Agree
C on the answer sheet = Neutral
D on the answer sheet = Disagree
E on the answer sheet = Strongly Disagree

Before beginning the actual scale, please write your social security number or any other number unique to you (for example, telephone number, birthdate) in the section on Side 1 of the NCS Answer Sheet entitled "Identification Number." This number will be used for data organization *only* and not for any other purpose. Your answers will be held in strict confidence. Please note that you will use *only* 147 answer blanks on the answer sheet.

1. _____ Rehabilitation and maintenance of deteriorating public housing should be the responsibility of the private sector.
2. _____ All direct-income benefits to welfare recipients should be in the form of cash.
3. _____ National health care programs should be made available only to those who cannot afford private health services.
4. _____ Social services should be concentrated in urban centers.
5. _____ Clients should have access to their records.
6. _____ It is impossible to take the needs of all recipients into account when planning for distribution of social services.
7. _____ Employment interviewers may question applicants about arrest records.
8. _____ National health care programs should include prevention programs as well as treatment.
9. _____ Foster care should always be time-limited.
10. _____ Immigrants should learn English as a prerequisite for U.S. citizenship.
11. _____ More attention should be given to the educational needs of children of migrant workers.
12. _____ More attention should be given to the educational needs of gifted children.
13. _____ When they are old enough, children should have the right to choose their religion, including the option to choose none.
14. _____ Banks should ease mortgage regulations in the low-income minority areas.
15. _____ Treatment programs should focus on the alcoholic's family as well as the alcoholic.
16. _____ The employed should have more government assistance than the unemployed.
17. _____ School breakfast and lunch programs are a waste of federal dollars.
18. _____ Sterilization is an acceptable method of reducing the welfare load.
19. _____ Counseling should be available to women who ask for abortions.
20. _____ There should be a guaranteed minimum income for everyone.
21. _____ Immigrants should receive unemployment benefits.
22. _____ Children are the property of their parents.

Appendix B   149

23. _____ Tax credits should not be given for child care.
24. _____ Couples should decide for themselves whether they want to become parents.
25. _____ The federal government has invested too much money in the poor.
26. _____ The government should not redistribute the wealth.
27. _____ Retirement at 65 should be mandatory.
28. _____ Marital rape should be outlawed in all states.
29. _____ Adoptees should have full information about their natural parents.
30. _____ The government should not interfere in the internal affairs of the family.
31. _____ Women should have the right to use abortion services.
32. _____ Immigrants should have the right to use their native language in all legal procedures.
33. _____ The dying have a right to be informed of their prognoses.
34. _____ Mothers of preschool children should not work outside the home.
35. _____ The FBI should keep files on individuals with minority political affiliation.
36. _____ National health services should be available to everyone.
37. _____ Abduction by parents who do not have custody should be viewed as a family, not a legal, matter.
38. _____ Women should have equal access to credit.
39. _____ The government should not subsidize family planning programs.
40. _____ Halfway houses should not be concentrated in the same geographic area.
41. _____ Children should not be entitled to due process.
42. _____ The availability of legal counsel should not depend on the ability to pay.
43. _____ The mandatory retirement age protects society from the imcompetence of the elderly.
44. _____ Abortion counseling should not be made available to teenagers without parental consent.
45. _____ Independent adoptions should be acceptable.
46. _____ Welfare mothers should be discouraged from having more children.

47. _____ Persons who work at home, performing household duties and caring for children, should be recognized as self-employed workers entitled to benefits similar to those employed outside the home.
48. _____ Revenue sharing with local governments provides a more equitable distribution of services.
49. _____ Unemployment benefits should not be available to pregnant women.
50. _____ Family planning should be available to all adolescents.
51. _____ Capital punishment should not be abolished.
52. _____ The government should provide a comprehensive system of insurance protection against loss of income because of disability.
53. _____ Unmarried pregnant women should receive abortion counseling.
54. _____ Immigrants should be given the right to obtain permanent resident visas without being forced to leave the United States.
55. _____ Mandatory retirement based on age should be eliminated.
56. _____ The assistance of law enforcement agencies, particularly the FBI, should be used to help locate children abducted by a parent.
57. _____ Everyone should have the right to good, adequate housing.
58. _____ Long-term care facilities should provide opportunities for sexual interactions for adults.
59. _____ Clients should have a right to be involved in the decision-making procedures of social agencies.
60. _____ Medicare adequately meets society's responsibility to provide medical care for the elderly.
61. _____ The death penalty is an important means for discouraging criminal activity.
62. _____ Local governments should be monitored on their enforcement of civil rights statutes.
63. _____ Confidential information about both parents should be given to adoptees only when questions of health are raised.
64. _____ Rural policies are more biased against women than are urban policies.
65. _____ The aged require only minimal mental health services.

Appendix B

66. _____ Welfare workers should keep files on those clients suspected of fraud.
67. _____ Information about clients can be shared with other professionals without the consent of the clients.
68. _____ Social intervention in the parent–child relationship should be undertaken only when the child's right to a secure home is seriously threatened.
69. _____ Experts in federal service should have greater input than local citizens in community planning.
70. _____ All services should be made available to AIDS victims and their families.
71. _____ Everyone should be protected from media influence on personal life-styles.
72. _____ Individuals should provide their own insurance against loss of income because of disability.
73. _____ Children have the right to legal counsel in court procedures affecting their interests.
74. _____ Only medical personnel should be involved in life and death treatment decisions.
75. _____ Pregnant adolescents should be excluded from school.
76. _____ More federal programs assist the rural poor than the urban poor.
77. _____ Those in need of long-term care should be maintained in the community as long as possible.
78. _____ Health care plans should cover alcohol- and drug-related conditions.
79. _____ Students should be denied government funds if they participate in protest demonstrations.
80. _____ Computerized data banks should ensure privacy.
81. _____ Society has a responsibility to help parents become more adequate in their parental roles.
82. _____ Volunteers should not be used to replace paid staff.
83. _____ Juveniles do not need to be provided with legal counsel in juvenile courts.
84. _____ Discrimination has been eliminated in most areas of employment.
85. _____ Corporal punishment is an important means of discipline for aggressive, acting-out adolescents.
86. _____ The poor can help themselves by working harder.

87. _____ Minority representation on police forces should be proportionate to minority representation in the community.
88. _____ Eligibility for a minimum income should be contingent on proven efforts to seek employment.
89. _____ Unemployment benefits should be extended, especially in areas hit by economic disaster.
90. _____ It would be better to give welfare recipients vouchers or goods rather than cash.
91. _____ Intoxication in public should be viewed as a crime.
92. _____ The gap between poverty and affluence should be reduced through measures directed at redistribution of income.
93. _____ The cost of child care should be subsidized by the community.
94. _____ Employers should not provide programs designed to improve family relations.
95. _____ A moratorium should be placed on construction of jails and prisons until alternative treatment measures have been implemented.
96. _____ The government should have primary responsibility for helping the community accept a returning offender.
97. _____ Efforts should be made to increase voting among minorities.
98. _____ Older persons should be involved in planning, developing, and administering programs for the elderly.
99. _____ Special efforts should be directed toward developing appropriate support services for adolescent parents.
100. _____ "No-knock" entry, which allows the police entrance without a search warrant, encourages police to violate the rights of individuals.
101. _____ Family planning services should be available to individuals regardless of income.
102. _____ Clients of public and voluntary agencies should be advised that their use of family planning services will in no way affect benefits they receive.
103. _____ Most offenders should have community-based treatment before any other form.
104. _____ Pregnant women over 40 should seek abortion services.
105. _____ Older persons should be sustained to the extent possible in their own environments.

106. _____ Economic aid for education should not be given to those who are readjusting to civilian life after military service.
107. _____ Mental health services should provide continuity of care and reduce unnecessary dependence on other services.
108. _____ Tokenism (selecting a few highly visible minorities), rather than genuine compliance with affirmative action, should remain the rule rather than the exception.
109. _____ The general welfare requires governmental participation in housing and community development.
110. _____ The child in adoption proceedings should be the primary client.
111. _____ Judges should be relieved of duties that are incompatible with their function as impartial decision makers.
112. _____ There should be no secret professional record-keeping systems.
113. _____ A family should be defined as two or more individuals who consider themselves a family and who assume protective, caring obligations to one another.
114. _____ Dying persons and their families should be involved in all treatment decisions.
115. _____ Alcoholism should be recognized as an illness, for which treatment planning, insurance coverage, and professional education are urgently needed.
116. _____ Teenage parents should be expected to assume the same responsibilities as older parents.
117. _____ Measures should be taken to encourage the employment of workers who are able to work beyond the age at which they become eligible for retirement.
118. _____ Cost containment measures should be applied to any system of national health care.
119. _____ Social workers who do not offer abortion counseling have no obligation to give referral information.
120. _____ Work hours should be adapted to meet the needs of families and handicapped individuals.
121. _____ Individuals who have committed illegal acts that do not constitute a threat to the community should be diverted by the courts from the criminal and juvenile justice systems to more appropriate sources of treatment.

Please select the most appropriate answer, and enter its letter on the NCF answer sheet.

122. Age:
- (a) under 25
- (b) 26–35
- (c) 36–45
- (d) 46–55
- (e) over 55

123. Gender:
- (a) male
- (b) female

124. Race:
- (a) Black
- (b) Caucasian
- (c) Hispanic
- (d) Chicano
- (e) other

125. Sexual preference:
- (a) heterosexual
- (b) gay/lesbian
- (c) bisexual

126. Marital status:
- (a) single
- (b) married
- (c) divorced
- (d) widowed
- (e) other

127. Number of children:
- (a) none
- (b) 1
- (c) 2–3
- (d) 4–5
- (e) more than 5

128. Current living arrangements:
- (a) living with parents
- (b) living with mate
- (c) living with mate/children
- (d) living alone
- (e) other

Appendix B

129. Political party affiliation:
- (a) Republican
- (b) Democrat
- (c) Independent
- (d) other
- (e) none

130. Political philosophy:
- (a) liberal
- (b) moderate
- (c) conservative
- (d) other

131. Political activity level:
- (a) totally uninterested; uninvolved in politics
- (b) sometimes vote in major elections
- (c) vote in most major elections; follow issues closely
- (d) actively campaign for candidates and social issues
- (e) have run for office; contribute $ to candidates

132. Religious affiliation:
- (a) Jewish
- (b) Protestant
- (c) Roman Catholic
- (d) other
- (e) none

133. Birthplace:
- (a) Northeast
- (b) South
- (c) Midwest
- (d) West
- (e) outside U.S.A.

134. Characteristics of birthplace:
- (a) rural
- (b) small town (fewer than 100,000)
- (c) mid-sized urban area (100,000–500,000)
- (d) suburban area near major metropolitan area
- (e) major metropolitan area (500,000 or more)

135. Current residence:
- (a) Northeast
- (b) South
- (c) Midwest
- (d) West
- (e) outside U.S.A.

136. Characteristics of current residence:
    (a) rural
    (b) small town (fewer than 100,000
    (c) mid-sized urban area (100,000–500,000)
    (d) suburban area near major metropolitan area
    (e) major metropolitan area (500,000 or more)
137. Current family income:
    (a) less than $14,999
    (b) $15,000–19,999
    (c) $20,000–29,999
    (d) $30,000–44,999
    (e) $45,000 or more
138. Father's educational level:
    (a) graduate/professional (postbaccalaureate)
    (b) college/university graduation
    (c) high school graduation
    (d) some high school
    (e) 8 or fewer years of education
139. Mother's educational level:
    (a) graduate/professional (postbaccalaureate)
    (b) college/university graduation
    (c) high school graduation
    (d) some high school
    (e) 8 or fewer years of education

POS was sent to the various groups that follow with different versions of the last page as specified:

Form A: social work students
        social work graduates

Form B: Students of:
        law
        business
        medicine
        psychology
        nursing
        sociology
        education

Appendix B 157

Form C: lawyers
　　　　　physicians
　　　　　psychologists
　　　　　nurses
　　　　　educators
　　　　　businesspeople
　　　　　NASW members

Form D: social work faculty
　　　　　field instructors
　　　　　agency personnel

Form A

Students: Answer 140 *or* 141 *and* 142 through 147.
Graduates: Go directly to 143 through 147.

140. If a *social work student,* major course of study:
    (a) MSW direct practice (casework/group work)
    (b) MSW administration/planning/policy
    (c) MSW health care
    (d) BASW/BSW
    (e) nonmatriculated
    Go directly to 142.

141. If a *non-*social work student, major course of study:
    (a) business
    (b) law
    (c) psychology/sociology
    (d) nursing
    (e) other

142. Number of credits earned by the end of the current semester:
    (a) 1–15
    (b) 16–30
    (c) 31–60
    (d) 61–90
    (e) 91+

143. Highest degree earned:
    (a) high school
    (b) associate's
    (c) bachelor's
    (d) master's
    (e) post-master's

144. Title of present position:
- (a) direct practitioner, caseworker, case aide
- (b) supervisor of direct practice
- (c) administrator of agency
- (d) consultant
- (e) other

145. Major method of expertise:
- (a) casework
- (b) group work
- (c) community organization
- (d) administration
- (e) other

146. Agency auspices:
- (a) private
- (b) public
- (c) combined
- (d) other

147. Number of years employed in profession:
- (a) 0–5
- (b) 6–10
- (c) 11–15
- (d) 16–20
- (e) 21+

Form B

140. Major professional affiliation:
- (a) law or education
- (b) social work
- (c) psychology
- (d) medicine or nursing
- (e) business

141. Degree toward which you are presently working:
- (a) JD, MD, or DO
- (b) MSW, MSS, or MA
- (c) PhD or DSW
- (d) MSN or MEd
- (e) MBA, BSN, BS, BA

142. Number of credits completed (1 year = 30 credits):
- (a) 1–15
- (b) 16–30
- (c) 31–60
- (d) 61–90
- (e) 90+

Appendix B 159

143. Highest degree earned:
- (a) high school
- (b) associate's
- (c) bachelor's
- (d) master's
- (e) post-master's

144. Number of years of work experience in positions related to your present field of study:
- (a) 0–5
- (b) 6–10
- (c) 11–15
- (d) 16+
- (e) none

145. Total number of years of work experience (including those indicated in item 144 above):
- (a) 0–5
- (b) 6–10
- (c) 11–15
- (d) 16–20
- (e) 20+

146. This scale covered the domain of current social issues adequately:
- (a) strongly agree
- (b) agree
- (c) neutral
- (d) disagree
- (e) strongly disagree

147. The items were stated with sufficient clarity:
- (a) strongly agree
- (b) agree
- (c) neutral
- (d) disagree
- (e) strongly disagree

Form C

140. Major professional affiliation:
- (a) law or education
- (b) social work
- (c) psychology
- (d) nursing or medicine
- (e) business

141. Highest degree earned:
    (a) JD, MD, DO
    (b) MSW, MSS, or MA
    (c) PhD or DSW
    (d) MSN or MEd
    (e) MBA, BSN, BA, or BS
142. Major work setting:
    (a) private, nonprofit
    (b) public, nonprofit
    (c) private, profit
    (d) other
143. Number of years employed in profession:
    (a) 0–5
    (b) 6–10
    (c) 11–15
    (d) 16–20
    (e) 21+
144. Major supervisory responsibilities:
    (a) supervise other employees, with no supervision of own work
    (b) supervise others, with ongoing supervision of own work
    (c) work independently, with no supervision or supervisory responsibilities
    (d) supervised regularly, with no supervisory responsibilities
    (e) none of the above
145. Occupation of majority of clients whom you serve:
    (a) professionals, executives, senior-level managers
    (b) administrative personnel, owners of small businesses, lower-level professionals
    (c) skilled workers, clerical/sales workers, technicians
    (d) unskilled workers
    (e) a variety of the above
146. This scale covered the domain of current social issues adequately:
    (a) strongly agree
    (b) agree
    (c) neutral
    (d) disagree
    (e) strongly disagree
147. Major professional association membership:
    (a) American Bar Association or National Educational Association
    (b) National Association of Social Workers or National Association of Manufacturers

Appendix B **161**

    (c) American Psychological Association or Association of MBA Executives
    (d) American Nurses' Association or American Medical Association
    (e) American Management Association

Form D

140. Highest degree earned:
    (a) high school
    (b) associate's
    (c) bachelor's
    (d) master's
    (e) doctorate
141. Degree earned in:
    (a) social work
    (b) psychology
    (c) sociology
    (d) mental health
    (e) other
142. Major job classification:
    (a) full-time social work faculty member
    (b) adjunct faculty member
    (c) field instructor
    (d) agency executive
    (e) agency board member
143. Major responsibility:
    (a) teaching
    (b) faculty field instruction coordination
    (c) administration
    (d) direct practice
    (e) supervision of others in direct practice
144. Major method of expertise:
    (a) casework
    (b) group work
    (c) community organization
    (d) administration and/or planning
    (e) other
145. Agency or university auspices:
    (a) private
    (b) public
    (c) combination
    (d) other

146. Number of years employed in present capacity:
    (a) 0–5
    (b) 6–10
    (c) 11–15
    (d) 16–20
    (e) 21+

147. Number of years employed in social work (including number of years listed above):
    (a) 0–7
    (b) 8–14
    (c) 15–22
    (d) 23–30
    (e) 31+

About the Author

Ann A. Abbott is both a social work educator and direct practitioner. Her research strongly reflects both capacities. She has directed both BSW and MSW programs and has served as a CSWE accreditation site visitor for numerous programs.

The author currently is chairperson of the Social Work Department at Rutgers—The State University, Camden Campus, where she teaches direct practice courses. Dr. Abbott's involvement with NASW has been extensive, including her current position as president of the Pennsylvania Chapter. She holds an MSW and DSW from Bryn Mawr College Graduate School of Social Work and Social Research.

Readers may contact Dr. Abbott for further information at P.O. Box 637, Villanova, PA 19085.

DATE DUE

12/3/94			
SE 21 '95			
DE 18 '98			

```
HV                    60551
11
.A19      Abbott, Ann Augustine
1988          Professional choices.
```

HIEBERT LIBRARY
Fresno Pacific College - M. B. Seminary
Fresno, Calif 93702

DEMCO